A **taste** of **Northumberland**

Traditional country cooking with Veronica Heath

PUBLISHED BY POWDENE PUBLICITY

Contents

First published in 2001 by

Powdene Publicity Ltd, Unit 17, St Peter's Wharf,

Newcastle upon Tyne NE6 1TZ. Telephone: (0191) 265 0040.

© Veronica Heath 2001.

British Library Cataloguing in Publication Data.

A catalogue record of this book is available from the British Library.

ISBN No. 0-9520226-4-8

Printed by: Reed Print & Design, Tyne & Wear.

Acknowledgements

Food photography – Barbara Berkowitz

Other photography – Douglas Hall, Powdene.

Drawings by John Steele

Photo assistance – The Real Cheese Shop, Morpeth.

   Hugh Lough, Butcher, Jesmond.

   Mark Robertson, Make-Me-Rich Cheese Farm.

   Chain Bridge Honey Farm, Horncliffe.

Introduction

MY recipes are all fairly simple. I don't have the time or inclination to spend hours fussing in the kitchen. Today, we all have to live many different lives and this is reflected in our cooking; one minute the cool host with food appearing as if by magic, next the harassed career woman – or man – trying to get a meal ready in no time flat.

We probably fall into and out of these categories week by week, but one thing is certain: we all have to eat, so why not enjoy our cooking? Anyway, I have become convinced that elaboration in cooking is usually self-defeating.

If you use ingredients which are the freshest and best of their kind – whether they be humble cabbage or leek, or the glorious grouse – simple good cooking will show them off to maximum advantage. Many of my recipes have been given to me by friends. I try them at home and, if we like them and they are practical to prepare, I pass them on to my readers.

Whatever recipes you choose for entertaining, remember that the idea is to make your guests and family happy, and to enable you to enjoy yourself without having to do too much hard work.

Instead of the cooking perfection of haute cuisine, go for quality ingredients which are easy to cook, possibly robust and gutsy, frequently from the freezer if that makes it easier – but always enjoyable.

VERONICA HEATH

Summer

The kitchen revels in fresh new vegetables, fish, combs of honey and soft fruit, so make the most of them during the all-too-short summer months.

We cannot do anything about the weather but, whenever possible, it's the season to enjoy picnics, barbecues and informal entertaining. Summer can be a hectic time for the cook with freezing and preserving in full swing, but at least there is not a problem deciding what to put on the menu when it comes to puddings.

Picnics

WHEN summer lives up to its name, the cook wants to spend as much time as possible out of doors and very little in the kitchen. But even planning a picnic for a day out in the country takes ingenuity and culinary skill to ensure that it is satisfying and delicious, without being stodgy or difficult to eat.

The Victorians understood the art of eating outdoors, but they had the staff to mastermind the operation. When Queen Victoria and her consort left the formality of the court for the freedom of Balmoral, each day's outing was planned around an outdoor luncheon transported up the highland tracks by minions. It must have taken a full staff to stow away the half-consumed spreads recommended by Mrs Beeton, not to mention the damask cloths, napkins, camping stools, wicker baskets and spirit lamps considered necessary.

Today, most of us have blenders or food processors to help make light work of the worst chores. A light hand is essential: rich and heavy foods are out. Remember the picnic adage — the grander the spread, the greater the potential disaster. No point in providing a loaded hamper so heavy that it takes four people to carry it. We want food that is easy to transport and even easier to eat.

When deciding on what to provide, remember that the visual appeal should vie with the gastronomic. Cold food can look unappetising and taste stodgy, so it must be selected with care. Avoid supplying too many choices. Two, or at most three, alternatives are all that is needed. The hostess wants to enjoy her day out too and there is little point taking 20 minutes to lay out a lunch which will likely need to be protected from the rain, the dogs or hungry children, and which your guests will consume in less than half an hour.

It sounds recklessly extravagant to cook a lean, boned piece of beef and serve it cold for picnics but it is always hugely popular. You can console yourself that it will go further cold and thinly sliced than it would as the Sunday joint. It's delicious with wholemeal bread or a French stick, and remember the jar of horseradish sauce. Lettuce in sandwiches tends to slip, so avoid it.

Pâté must be served with rolls of crusty bread for guests to spread themselves. Pâté in a sandwich doesn't taste the

same. Quiches tend to break or crumble if they are not handled with extreme care and then often taste soggy. Cornish pasties are better, but too much cold pastry on a hot day is stodgy, especially for children.

Meat loaf is one of my picnic stand-bys, especially if we are having a knife and fork meal with salad. I use a recipe I learned in a class at Kirkley Hall years ago and it never lets me down.

Devilled chicken is always a wow — made with cream it sounds recklessly expensive, but a little goes a long way and it has the advantage that it can be made in advance to improve it when left in the fridge. Serve in a large round carton or in individual yoghurt pots, and provide spoons or thick carrot sticks to eat it with.

Real lemonade is easy to make and wonderfully thirst-quenching: include plenty of lemon zest to give it a refreshing zing. Lemon barley water is another home-made favourite — allow 50 g/2 oz sugar, 110 g/4 oz pearl barley and 4 lemons to 2 pints of water.

CUCUMBER SOUP

Ingredients:

1 large cucumber;
1 stock cube (chicken, fish or vegetable);
1 1/2 teaspoons Tarragon or white wine vinegar;
1 teaspoon caster sugar;
450 ml/15 fl oz/3/4 pint of quality, creamy yoghurt;
fresh dill;
1/2 teaspoon salt.

Peel, halve and scoop out the seeds from the cucumber. Discard the seeds and reserve the peel. Cut the flesh into fine shreds, dissolve the stock cube in 1/4 pint of boiling water and stir in vinegar, caster sugar and salt. Put the stock into a blender, add the cucumber peel and process until you have a green-flecked purée.

Strain the liquid through a sieve, pressing the tiny shreds of cucumber peel with a wooden spoon to get every drop of green liquid from it. Slowly stir the yoghurt into the green liquid, then stir in the finely shredded cucumber flesh and chopped dill. Cover and chill for several hours before serving to allow the flavours to infuse.

DEVILLED CHICKEN

Ingredients:

1 chicken;
110 g/1/4 lb butter;
3 tablespoons good oil;
1 cup of double cream;
2 tablespoons mango chutney;
2 tablespoons Worcestershire sauce;
1 1/2 tablespoons curry powder.

Pre-heat the oven to 400 deg F/200 deg C/Gas 6. Put the bird in to bake with the butter smeared over it and the oil hot in the dish. Turn the oven down to 350 deg F/180 deg C/ Gas 4.

After 10 minutes turn it on to its breast and baste regularly. Don't overcook. When the bird is cold, cut the meat off the carcase and chop it into bite-size pieces. Whip the cream lightly until smooth but not too stiff. Add the chutney, Worcestershire sauce and curry powder to the cream, also some black pepper. Put the chicken pieces into the creamy mix and turn it into a suitable container for carrying.

Serves 6 to 8.

Ingredients:
900 g/2 lb good minced beef;
3 large slices of bread;
2 eggs;
1 medium onion;
1 teaspoon dry mustard;
1 tablespoon tomato ketchup;
1 tablespoon horseradish sauce;
1 tablespoon soy sauce;
2 teaspoons chopped parsley;
1 teaspoon mixed herbs;
1 medium green pepper, de-seeded and chopped small;
2 level teaspoons salt and some black pepper;
1 tablespoon porridge oats.

Break the bread into chunks and put it into a blender with the eggs, onion, green pepper, mustard, sauces and seasonings. Mix until this becomes a smooth paste. Turn it into a bowl, add the oats and the mince. Beat thoroughly and then shape it all into a loaf tin, or two loaf tins. Bake at 425 deg F/220 deg C/ Gas 7 for 10 minutes and then turn the oven down to 350 deg F/180 deg C/Gas 4 and leave for about another 40 minutes.

You can line the tins with bacon as this helps to hold it together. When it is warm but not yet cold, sprinkle breadcrumbs over the loaf to finish. Serve cold in slices. This loaf will freeze.

Pâté

BRITISH taste-buds, not to mention British imagination, have been broadened by time and travel. The word 'pâté' now embraces a wide-ranging selection of foods — fish and vegetables as well as meat. It can have a variety of textures and can be served on all sorts of occasions.

Personal opinions differ widely, so it is difficult to commit oneself on how the perfect pâté should taste, but the criterion is that a good pâté — like a good wine — must be given time to ripen and mellow.

I have noticed that if we eat a pâté or a terrine over a period of several days, it is usually much the best just when it is being finished up.

Which spirits you mix in is a matter of taste: port and madeira are in many recipes, but I like brandy and wine, and some don't need booze at all.

Pâté does seem to be a foreign import, primarily French, with every charcuterie worthy of the name having its own recipe for *pâté de campagne* and many cooks having their own secrets. The basic mix is pork but other meats can be included, particularly game and poultry.

You only have to sit on a canal bank in France with a glass of something red and fruity, a stick of bread and a wedge of country pâté to know that you have arrived. No meal during the holiday will taste as good.

The best pâté I have ever eaten was bought in the Languedoc. Maybe it was the way Madame rubbed the pan in brandy, the sheer freshness of the chicken livers or the 10 tablespoons of butter. Anyway, it tasted home-made — which is the first, last and best word on the subject.

Pâtés freeze, but benefit from being slowly and thoroughly thawed. The rich, creamy kind taste much better when served at room temperature, soft and smooth and with flavours fully developed.

Rough pâtés do not freeze well, tending to acquire a slightly wet texture in the freezer, but you can prepare your mixture ahead and freeze it uncooked for a few weeks.

Pâtés can be sliceable, spreadable, even dippable, and need not necessarily be accompanied with butter and toast. They are very good eaten with oatcakes or celery sticks, or crusty bread, or you can make a meal of it with baked potatoes and salad.

A genuine taste for lighter foods is emerging today, but only a killjoy would rule a rich meat pâté out of their lives completely. But I would not now serve a meat or game pâté as an entrée before a main course with meat — a menu pattern which was commonplace only 20 years ago.

Fish pâtés have gained many fans and are easy to make. Our younger son is a fisherman and he always has a glut of trout in his freezer which he off-loads on to me to make pâtés and pies.

Once the freezer's rapacious maw has swallowed up a dish it is easy to forget which ingredients are necessary to finish it off on thawing. Parsley, bay leaves or a sprinkle of sesame seeds can be forgotten, so write any finishing instructions on the labels before freezing to remind you.

Here are three of my favourite pâté recipes.

ROUGH COUNTRY PÂTÉ

Ingredients:
350 g/³/₄ lb pork fillet;
110 g/¹/₄ lb pig's liver or roedeer liver (if you can get it);
450 g/1 lb fresh spinach (or 9 oz frozen whole leaf spinach);
juice of one orange, and a small amount of orange zest;
garlic, coriander seeds and thyme;
redcurrant jelly;
6-8 long thin streaky bacon rashers.

Chop the pork and the liver roughly, and then process to give a fairly coarse texture. Stir in the grated zest of the orange and one tablespoon of juice. Add two garlic cloves that have been crushed with one teaspoon of salt and one teaspoon of coriander seeds, one teaspoon of dried thyme and a good grinding of pepper.

I like a tablespoon of redcurrant jelly, but this is optional. Cover and leave the mixture in a cold place for several hours, or overnight to allow the flavours to blend.

Cook the spinach, drain it and let it become cold. Squeeze it to extract as much liquid as possible, then chop it finely and mix it with the pork. De-rind the bacon and stretch with the back of a knife. Oil a terrine dish and line it criss-cross fashion with the rashers of bacon. Pack the pork and spinach mixture into the dish and fold the ends of bacon over the top.

Cover the dish with oiled foil, stand it in a roasting tin containing freshly boiled water halfway up the sides of the pâté dish and put the pan in the oven at approximately 325 deg F/170 deg C/Gas 3 for about 1¹/₂ hours. When the pâté is cooked, leave it in the tin until it is cold; this will make it easier to slice for serving.

HAM AND MUSTARD PÂTÉ

Ingredients:
2.2 kg/5 lb chicken livers;
700 g/1¹/₂ lb ham (raw);
1 tablespoon garlic purée;
2 tablespoons wholegrain mustard;
salt and pepper;
275 g/10 oz butter and 275 g/10 oz margarine;
300 ml/10 fl oz/¹/₂ pint double cream;
3 tablespoons brandy.

Easy and very delicious. Roughly chop the ham and livers and then process them with the other ingredients. Add the cream and brandy and process again until you get the required texture. Cool and decorate.

PANNA

(Mrs Kenneth Clark's recipe)
Ingredients:
a handful of spinach;
1 onion;
2 hard-boiled eggs;
1 piece of tarragon and a bunch of parsley;
3 or 4 sardines and some anchovies;
a large knob of butter.

Boil the spinach, the finely-chopped onion, the tarragon and the parsley until cooked. Press or squeeze out all the water.

Have the hard-boiled eggs, the sardines, the anchovies and the butter ready and pound or blend all together, and then pass through a sieve. Spread thickly. Season well, then pack into a flat dish and serve with hot toast. Panna makes excellent sandwiches if you have any over.

—Shellfish—

WITH tidal water within reach of all of us in this county, and tumbling streams and rivers even closer, it is not surprising that fish and crustaceans have made such a mark on our cooking.

Shellfish from our North East coast have been popular food since prehistoric times, and in medieval times made a welcome change from the monotonous diet of salt fish endured during the period when obligatory fish eating was imposed by the church.

A fisherman in Seahouses told me that the cold water of the north Atlantic firms and sweetens the flesh of crabs and lobsters like no other sea water. Along with Scandinavia, we have the best crustaceans in Europe and, provided they are fresh, the lily needs no gilding.

Last time that I was at Amble there were crates of fresh crabs and lobsters being brought on shore, and I spent an informative hour with a knowledgeable fellow who knew his crustaceans. Shellfish must be eaten as fresh as possible; you can tell a lobster is fresh if the tail springs back when it is pulled. Choose one weighing about a pound and a half which feels heavy for its size.

Live lobsters are dark blue, but turn bright red and orange when they are boiled. Crabs should have stiff claws attached — if you shake one and hear the sound of water inside the shell, do not buy it. Prawns may be sold boiled, shelled or

unshelled, while shrimps are generally sold cooked in their shells.

For years I resisted dressing crabs and lobsters — far too much trouble — but provided you have time on your side, preparing shellfish is not difficult, although it is messy. If you don't feel up to the task, ask a fishmonger to do it for you.

13

LOBSTER WITH MAYONNAISE

Allowing one lobster per person, place them in a pan of lukewarm water, cover and bring to the boil. Cook for 10 minutes, or until they no longer have any blue hue and assume an orange-reddish colour.

Remove the lobsters from the pan and leave to cool. Then, with a sharp knife, make an incision at the point where the head joins the body and cut down the length of the lobster's back towards the tail. Make sure that you have cut right the way through the body.

Now turn the lobster 180 degrees and cut from the original incision back through the head. With your fingers, gradually prise the shell apart so that it falls into two halves. Remove the front claws and set aside. With your index finger prise the meat out of the shell, trying to keep it in one piece, again working from the tail upwards. Then replace the meat in the shell (which makes it easier for the diners to keep their fingers clean) and repeat with the second half.

Using a hammer, crack both sides of the claws, remove the surrounding shell and extract the meat in a single piece. Arrange the two halves of lobster on a plate together with the claw meat and serve with mayonnaise, preferably home-made.

BOILED CRAB

Ingredients:
Crab(s) about 1 kg/2 lb in weight;
3.8 litres/6 pints water;
225 g/8 oz salt.

Fill a saucepan with sea water if possible, using only 4 oz of salt, or 8 oz if you have to use ordinary tap water. Tie the crab's claws and put it in the pan while the water is cold, bringing gently to the boil. As soon as the water boils, hold the crab under so that it has a quick death, if it is unfortunate enough to still be alive.

Boil for 15 minutes for the first pound and 10 minutes for each subsequent pound in weight. Let the crab cool in the water, then lift it out and pull the body from the shell. Remove the ring of feathery grey and snap off the mouth part. Everything else is edible.

Eat with fingers or a fork. You need a sharp instrument for picking the meat out of the claws. Fresh crab goes well with a dish of boiled potatoes and some butter, but slices of brown bread, lettuce and mayonnaise do equally well.

PRAWNS

Ingredients:
900 g/2 lb fresh prawns;
3 tablespoons butter;
juice of one lemon and some salt.

Steam the prawns in a colander over boiling water for about 20 minutes. Leave them to cool a few minutes and then shell them by holding the head between the thumb and forefinger of your right hand and the tail with the left hand; gently pinch and pull off the tail shells. Hold the body while you carefully pull off the head, the soft body shell and the small claws.

Melt the butter gently in a frying pan, not letting it get brown. Add the prawns to the pan and shake gently in the butter. Sprinkle them lightly with salt and then add the lemon juice, stirring to mix them well together.

Cook for a few minutes until the butter becomes a faint pink, then eat with bread and butter. Frozen prawns are suitable for prawn cocktails and deep frying.

Trout

FISH provides, pound for pound, slightly more protein than meat. River fish — salmon and trout — are described as game fish and are now widely sold commercially, with rainbow trout raised in fish farms the most widely sold trout.

I would always go for burn or brown trout in place of farmed trout; there is a difference in texture and flavour although with improved feeding the difference is not as marked as it was. If buying from a trout farm, notice whether the water in the tanks is both running and clear because if the fish are swimming in dirty water they can taste muddy.

Like vegetables, trout are best served straight from oven or pan as soon as they are cooked. The cook should not think of starting until the fisherman has changed out of his waders and is ready to sit down at table. Gipsies, who knew more about cooking trout than most of us, boiled their catch from the burn — often caught by groping or tickling rather than by more orthodox methods — over a fire of sticks and peat turf.

One of the most delicious ways to present fresh trout is to wrap the cleaned fish in some wet newspaper, well soaked. Bake the bundle in the oven until the newspaper feels quite dry, about 15-20 minutes. Unwrap and eat. A simple method, but delicious.

The trout angler must learn to clean his own fish. With a

sharp knife, slit the belly from the vent to the throat and remove all the intestines. Cut off the fins if you plan to use the trout for a party. Then wash the trout under the cold water tap.

When I have had a surfeit of trout and the family have got tired of my simple, traditional methods of serving them, I make kedgeree *(see Page 51)* using skinned, cooked trout. There are bones, but I spend a few moments removing all I can find and have no complaints. Every morsel in the dish gets eaten and kedgeree is particularly nice for breakfast when friends or family are staying with us.

Smoked trout is very good, and although the fish is closely related to salmon, the two do not taste at all alike. The flesh of smoked trout is pink or white, and firm, the taste subtle and lacking the oiliness of the larger fish.

Smoked trout makes a good starter and should be served with horseradish sauce, lemon and brown bread and butter.

Classic methods of cooking trout are as follows:

TROUT MEUNIÈRE

Ingredients:
allow a 300 g/10-12 oz trout per person;
flour;
salt and pepper;
60 g/2-3 oz butter;
lemon wedges to garnish.

Clean the fish and wash and dry them well. Season and then roll in flour, shaking off any surplus. Melt the butter in a heavy-based pan and as soon as it foams, lay in the trout and cook gently, turning the fish over as soon as the underside is browned. The trout will be done when a little flesh lifts gently from the head and comes away cleanly from the bone. Serve at once in its cooking juices with lemon wedges to garnish.

TROUT MOUSSE

Ingredients:
900 g/2 lb trout;
150 ml/5 fl oz/¹/4 pint mayonnaise;
150 ml/5 fl oz/¹/4 pint bechamel sauce;
75 g/3 oz butter;
300 ml/10 fl oz/¹/2 pint whipped cream;
25 g/1 oz gelatine;
¹/2 cup white wine.

A surfeit of trout can be cooked and transformed into pâté or mousse. A mousse is easy to make but care must be taken to remove all the bones. Poach the fish, then discard the skin and bones and mash the flesh or whizz it up in a blender until it is smooth. Add the butter and lastly the gelatine dissolved in half a cup of white wine. Fold in the cream lightly whipped. Turn the mix into a mould or soufflé dish and garnish with lemon and slices of cucumber to serve.

TROUT AU GRATIN

Ingredients:

4 freshly caught, filleted trout;
150 ml/5 fl oz/¹/2 pint dry white wine;
150 ml/5 fl oz/¹/2 pint water;
seasoning;
butter;
175 g/6 oz mushrooms;
110 g/¹/4 lb frozen prawns;
150 ml/5 fl oz/¹/4 pint double cream;
2 egg yolks;
4 tablespoons grated Gruyère cheese.

Poach the trout in a court bouillon (a seasoned stock) made of equal parts of wine and water, season to taste with salt and freshly ground black pepper. Transfer the fillets to a warmed, well-buttered oven-proof dish and keep warm. Add four tablespoons of butter, sliced mushrooms and prawns to the sauce and bring to the boil. Cook over heat until the sauce is reduced to about half its original quantity. Remove from the heat and combine the double cream and egg yolks in a small bowl. Stir in a little of the hot sauce, then pour the egg and cream mixture into the hot sauce and cook over a medium heat, stirring constantly until the mixture thickens. Avoid letting it come to the boil or it may curdle. Pour the sauce over the filleted trout and sprinkle with grated Gruyère and then put under the grill until the sauce is bubbly and golden.

Summer Fruits

THE harvest of delicious fruits in our gardens and in the pick-your-own farms signals such a good time for the cook.

When scarlet berries, currants and cherries first come into season they are so delicious that it is unnecessary to adorn them. We feast on strawberries, raspberries and red and blackcurrants plain and simple, and when there is too much of a glut I start slicing, crushing and whipping the fruits into sweet summer puddings.

But at first, we want nothing better than to eat them just as they are, so that their colours, shapes and luscious juiciness can be enjoyed to the full. The deep freeze is a boon: how did we preserve our fruit and veg before it came into our lives? I suspect, alas, that much garden produce was wasted.

In midsummer, remember that simple soft fruit dishes should be stunning in their simplicity. You can afford to be generous, because there will not be any wastage. Fruit served on the stalk retains its freshness well, and any that is not eaten can be re-used in other dishes such as mousses and fools.

Fresh cream is the classic accompaniment to summer fruit, but if you find cream on its own too rich and cloying, you can lighten the richness by mixing cream with either whisked egg white or with yoghurt. Too much bland cream will mask the fruitiness of fresh fruit and flavourings can overpower rather than enhance, if used indiscriminately.

If you use a recipe which includes Kirsch or orange Curaçao, add it sparingly. A spoonful of liqueur is good news, a glassful a mistake.

Gooseberries ripen before other English fruits, almost a month ahead of strawberries in the North East. Gooseberry fool is always popular and freezes well in cartons. The word 'fool' in this context has nothing to do with foolishness but is derived from the French word *fouler* — to crush.

GOOSEBERRY FOOL

Ingredients:
700 g/1 1/2 lb gooseberries;
110 g/4 oz sugar;
2 tablespoons water;
300 ml/10 fl oz/1/2 pint double cream, whipped;
300 ml/10 fl oz/1/2 pint custard.

Put the topped and tailed gooseberries in a pan with the water and sugar and simmer for a couple of minutes until the gooseberries become soft, but not mushy. Put them into a blender, then fold in the whipped cream and the custard and turn into a serving dish. The idea of the custard is to make a larger pudding and prevent the sweet becoming too sharp-tasting. If you want to omit the custard, add more sugar. Chill until ready to serve.

Serves 4 to 6.

RASPBERRY VELVET TART

If you have children to feed, try this tart, which is equally good made with strawberries or peaches and always goes down well.

Ingredients:

rich flan pastry (175 g/6 oz plain and 50 g/2 oz self-raising flour, 110 g/4 oz butter, 60 g/2^{1}/2 oz caster sugar and half an egg);
225 g/8 oz white chocolate;
75 ml/3 fl oz whipping cream;
10 g/^{1}/2 oz butter;
350 g/12 oz raspberries, strawberries or peaches.

Make the pastry and line an 8-inch flan tin. Bake blind and then cool completely. Melt the chocolate carefully over hot water and mix in the warmish cream and butter. Distribute the fruit over the flan case, pour the chocolate mixture over and put in the fridge until firm. Decorate with extra fruit and/or chocolate leaves, or distribute a milk chocolate flake over the top.

STRAWBERRY MOUSSE

A mousse is impressive for entertaining and special occasions.

Ingredients:

225 g/8 oz strawberries;
3 egg yolks and 2 egg whites;
1 oz caster sugar;
150 ml/5 fl oz/^{1}/4 pint double or whipping cream;
toasted flaked almonds.

This recipe is ideal for using overripe strawberries. Mix them in the blender or sieve them. Whisk the egg yolks, sugar and strawberry purée in a pan over just-boiling water until thick. Remove from the heat and whisk until cool. Lightly whip the cream, then fold it into the strawberry mixture. Whisk the egg whites and fold them in. Tip into a large serving bowl or individual glasses and chill.

Decorate with toasted flaked almonds. This mousse is best made on the morning that it is to be eaten.

——— Honey ———

IN the sixth century BC, the philosopher Pythagoras recommended honey to his followers as an aid to good health and an elixir for a long life.

Centuries later, the Romans on Hadrian's Wall were eating honey cake, a popular delicacy to which they sometimes added figs and nuts.

In general terms, honey refers to a product from the honey bee *(apis mellifica)* and is, in its raw state, a nectar of flowers carried in the bee's crop or honey bag where it is acted upon by a ferment which modifies its character.

When its crop is full, the bee returns to the hive and regurgitates the contents. Honey is stored in the waxen cells of combs provided for the purpose and, to encourage the bees to collect a surplus in excess of their own needs, the beekeeper removes the combs as they are filled and substitutes empty sections.

To a considerable extent, the flavour of the produce depends upon the flowers that have been visited when each particular section of a comb has been filled. Individual worker bee cells are only about one fifth of an inch in diameter, with the cells of the drones and queens (the royal cells) being slightly larger.

Beekeepers used to keep their apiaries in dome-shaped straw hives known as skeps, but these have now been universally abandoned in favour of wooden hives on the bar-frame principle. When the population of a hive increases to capacity, part of it, headed by the old queen, issues forth as a swarm while the rest stay in the hive with a young queen reared for the purpose.

In a good summer there can be numerous swarms in one season. Bees require feeding in winter with sugar and glucose and need to be kept warm and dry. Northumberland is good honey country, with its grassland full of indigenous wild white clover and heather close enough for beekeepers to transport their hives to the moors in late summer months.

Our villages are prolific in robust spring flowers and blossom, and there are good winter quarters which can be selected for shelter and the provision of pollen such as willows, alders and wallflowers.

HONEY CAKE

This moist cake sometimes sinks a little in the middle but this in no way spoils the flavour. The Welsh make it with their local honey and cinnamon and the Scots use heather honey. I have found it most successful with clear, runny honey.

Ingredients:
110 g/4 oz honey;
75 g/3 oz butter;
75 g/3 oz sugar;
2 beaten eggs;
225 g/8 oz self-raising flour;
1 teaspoon baking powder;
50 g/2 oz ground almonds.

Cream the butter and sugar together and gradually beat in the eggs and honey. Add the sieved flour and the baking powder a little at a time and then the ground almonds. Mix well. Put the mixture into a greased and lined tin about nine inches in diameter and bake in a pre-heated oven for 45 minutes at 350 deg F/180 deg C/Gas 4.

HONEY AND BANANA ICE CREAM

Ingredients:
175 g/6 oz mashed banana;
2 tablespoons honey;
1 tablespoon lemon juice;
150 g/5 oz natural yoghurt;
1 egg white.

Mash or liquidise the bananas until they are smooth, then blend in the honey, lemon juice and yoghurt. Pour the mix into a freezer tray or a plastic box and freeze for one or two hours. Then beat well to remove any ice crystals. Whisk the egg white until it is stiff but not dry and carefully fold it into the banana mixture, starting with just a little and gradually adding the remainder. Spoon into the freezer tray or box, cover and return to the freezer until the ice cream is firm.

HONEYED LAMB

The marriage of lamb and honey is a particularly happy one, especially with a few herbs added to bring out the subtle flavour of the dish.

Ingredients:
1.8 kg/4 lb shoulder of lamb;
110 g/4 oz honey;
450 ml/15 fl oz/³/₄ pint of dry cider;
25 g/1 oz plain flour;
1 teaspoon lemon juice;
1 teaspoon chopped mint;
1¹/₂ teaspoons chopped thyme;
1 clove of garlic;
salt and pepper.

Line a roasting tin with foil large enough to wrap over the top of the joint. Rub the meat all over with the clove of garlic. Put the joint in the tin and season with salt and pepper. Mix the honey with half a pint of cider and pour over the joint. Sprinkle with the mint and thyme. Fold the foil loosely over the joint and cook in pre-heated oven for 30 minutes at 450 deg F/230 deg C/ Gas 8. Then open the foil parcel and baste with the rest of the cider. Close up the foil again, reduce the oven temperature to 350 deg F/180 deg C/Gas 4 and cook for another hour, folding back the foil to brown the meat after 30 minutes. New potatoes sprinkled with mint are delicious with honeyed lamb.

Serves 8 to 10.

Autumn

Living in the North East, we may have chilly weather as early as September, but this season provides ample compensation with an excuse for forays into the fields for mushrooms and hedgerow brambles.

Apples, beans and root vegetables keep the cook busy, and there are grouse and pheasant in abundance. Local pheasants are widely available and can be bought ready plucked and cleaned from butchers and fish shops. Make the most of them as a tasty alternative to chicken.

Autumn——
——Fruits

IN Northumberland, blackberries are most commonly found in hedges. Provided that you do not damage land or property, anyone can pick wild produce for their own use, except from nature reserves or land owned by the National Trust.

However, all common land belongs to someone, and owners are entitled to order you off their land for trespass. If you remove bushes or attempt to sell the produce, you risk prosecution for stealing!

Fortunately, brambles grow in abundance in field hedges and in local lanes and, despite ruthless mechanical hedge trimmers, my hands throughout every autumn are scratched and stained red from bramble picking expeditions. Put on your wellies, take a stick with a crook handle with you, and pull down the long suppliant tendrils whose entire length will be covered with thorns.

Blackberries are described in the Highlands as 'blessed brambles', but wild fruit is comparatively rare in hill country. A ghillie in the Deeside area tells me that his

family still uses the leaves to soothe burns and bruises, and he remembers his grandmother making dye from the fruit. Gather wild rose-hips to combine in a jelly and you get a bitter-sweet, purple confection — very good on buttered toast.

BRAMBLE SORBET

This simple sorbet recipe has proved popular with my family and visitors. Put 2 lb of brambles in a pan and cook, covered, over a gentle heat until the juices run, then cool and purée in a blender. Leave to cool completely.

In another pan, dissolve 1 lb caster sugar and one pint of water, then boil for $7\frac{1}{2}$ minutes. Cool the sugary mix and combine with the bramble purée, then put it in a polythene box container in the freezer. When it is freezing around the edges and beginning to form crystals, remove, scoop the contents back into the blender and whizz. Refreeze.

Repeat this twice more. The sorbet will become smooth and does not set hard because of the amount of sugar and it is easily scooped out, straight from the deep freeze when you want to eat it.

It sounds a lengthy process, but you do not need to wash the blender between each exercise and the work is easily combined with other cooking jobs, much like the routine on a baking day. This is a popular accompaniment to meat and game, but it is unusual and may not appeal to all diners.

BLACKBERRY WINE is another favourite with its rich, port-like flavour. Wine was not made from garden and hedgerow fruits in Britain until the late 17th century, because sugar was almost unobtainable before that date.

MUSHROOM SOUP

Depending on the weather, early autumn brings mushrooms and chanterelles. We are fortunate to have 'old' land, unturned by the plough, and the presence of manure from horses and cattle refreshes the organic content on which the mycelia of the fungus can thrive. All the same, there does seem to be a certain amount of luck about the appearance of field mushrooms in abundance.

With fungi, be sure that you know what you are picking to eat — some are deadly. If in doubt, use a field guide.

I make quantities of this soup with plants picked fresh.

The wind, the rain and the sun are elements which give a tang that the best cultivated mushrooms simply cannot match. Do not peel field mushrooms because much of the flavour lies in the skin, although a few which are dirty or flecked with manure will have to be peeled.

My soup recipe entails butter, sliced onion, garlic, chicken stock and thinly sliced mushrooms. I sometimes add cream or yoghurt before serving. It is a cheap and delicious picnic or supper dish with an interesting grainy texture. Garnish with one or two thinly sliced small mushrooms floating on the top.

WINDFALL CHUTNEY

This is a good recipe for making use of windfall fruit. Apples, pears and plums blend happily with green tomatoes to provide an ideal chutney as a complement to cold meats or cheese.

Ingredients:

1.1 kg/2$^{1}/_{2}$ lb apples, peeled and cored;
1.1 kg/2$^{1}/_{2}$ lb pears, peeled and cored;
1.1 kg/2$^{1}/_{2}$ lb stoned plums;
900 g/2 lb onions, peeled and chopped;
900 g/2 lb green tomatoes, washed and quartered;
220 g/8 oz mixed seedless raisins and sultanas;
450 g/1 lb marrow flesh, cut in half-inch cubes;
850 ml/28 fl oz/1$^{1}/_{2}$ pints malt vinegar;
50 ml/2 oz pickling spice, tied in a muslin bag;
225 g/8 oz soft brown sugar;
50 g/2 oz salt.

Do not use any bruised portions of the apples, pears and plums and chop the sound fruit into small chunks. Put all the prepared fruit into a large pan with the chopped onions, tomatoes, dried fruit and cubed marrow flesh. Add half the vinegar and spices tied in the bag.

Bring to the boil, then simmer until tender and pulpy, stirring occasionally. Add the sugar, salt and the rest of the vinegar, stirring until the sugar dissolves. Cook gently, stirring from time to time until the chutney becomes thick. Remove the spices, pot and seal. Leave to mature for about one month.

APPLE SNOW

This light sweet is meant to be tart, so resist the temptation to sweeten it too much.

Ingredients:
1.3 kg/3 lb apples (preferably Bramleys);
150 ml/5 fl oz/$^{1}/_4$ pint sweet cider;
75 g/3 oz caster sugar;
3 egg whites;
grated chocolate or cinnamon to garnish.

Peel, core and thinly slice the apples and cook these gently over a low heat with the cider until the fruit is soft and pulpy. Stir occasionally while these cook, then cook more quickly, stirring frequently until the apples are reduced to a foam. This drives a good deal of the moisture off.

Draw the pan off the heat and stir in the sugar, leave it to cool and then process the fruit to a thick smooth purée. Put the purée into a bowl and leave to become quite cold; do not cover. Whisk the egg whites until they stand in soft peaks, fold in the cold purée and spoon the apple snow into individual dishes or glasses. Before serving, scatter some ground cinnamon or grated chocolate on top.

——Grouse——

THANKS to our proximity to the wonderful grouse moors on the Northumberland/Durham borders, there has not yet been a season when I have not been given a few brace of grouse.

Contrary to common belief, it is not strictly necessary to hang a young grouse — either don't hang at all or hang for at least four days: the weather must dictate.

A week or longer is preferable for old birds, but if it is sultry the flies will immediately attack. Should you be given grouse as a present and suspect they are too high, pluck at once and wash the birds in vinegar. It does not spoil the taste and saves wasting a treat.

After years of experimentation in the kitchen, I have come to the conclusion that it is hard to create original ways to cook grouse. A lovely bird to cook, a young roast grouse is superb.

It is difficult when writing down recipes for roast game birds to convey how much watching, basting and cooking time to give a bird. Recipes should not be slavishly followed but considered only as a guide. Whatever game fowl you are presented with, experience and perfect young birds to cook are really the secret of success.

Grouse have delicate skins and need to be carefully plucked to prevent injury from ripping.

Adult grouse shed their toenails in late summer, so if a nail is detached it is a sure sign of an old bird. Young grouse have clean claws, smooth legs, no moulting ridge and the tip of the breastbone is readily pliable. An old bird, a cock, has well defined wattles. Put him in a pie or, better still, in the grouse pudding recipe (opposite page).

The feet should be removed from the bird for roasting. Cut through the bone from the front below the drumstick joint, pull off the foot and the lower leg, drawing the tendons from the drumstick. Barding a bird means seasoning it and laying a piece of fat bacon or substitute over the breast and tying it on with string. Smear cranberry jam or jelly on the bacon side next to the grouse to keep it moist; they spoil by becoming dry.

Bread sauce is traditionally served with grouse but I rarely do this now. The tradition of this accompaniment must have originated because it is a bland sauce to compliment a bird which used to be served rather high so that it tasted gamey. A young grouse will need about 40 minutes in a pre-set oven at 400 deg F/200 deg C/Gas 6. Serve it with a thin gravy made from the pan juices and, preferably, game chips.

After years of cooking game I find that it is always recipes from friends which I rely upon. Homely dishes with carefully chosen flavours, blended together, correctly cooked and presented. A friend in Hexham, Mrs Kenneth Clark, gave me this grouse pudding, a succulent, buttery dish and a treasure for anyone with old grouse to use:

GROUSE PUDDING

Ingredients:
2 grouse of uncertain age;
1 quartered onion;
4 crushed juniper berries;
bouquet garni, salt and pepper;
225 g/8 oz self-raising flour;
75 g/3 oz butter;
1 teaspoon finely grated lemon rind;
3 tablespoons iced water;
2 tablespoons plain flour;
175 g/6 oz sliced mushrooms;
1 egg yolk;
1 peeled and sliced eating apple.

Cut off each breast and divide into three, then cut off as much of the rest of the meat as possible. Break up the carcase and put it in a pan with onion and juniper berries and bouquet garni, add 1½ pints of water.

To make the crust, sift the flour with salt and pepper, dice the butter into the flour and rub it in. Combine the egg yolk with iced water, mix and sprinkle over flour mix and toss together with a fork. Using hands, knead lightly into a ball and roll the dough out on a board to fit a 2½ pint pudding basin, trim off and keep a piece for the lid.

Toss the grouse flesh in seasoned flour, combine with apple and mushrooms and pack into a basin. Pour in stock to come two-thirds up the filling. Damp edges and press on lid. Then steam for 2½ hours. Just before serving, cut a hole in the top and pour in a little more stock.

Another Northumbrian friend of mine makes very acceptable pâté which we spread on toast by mixing minced, cooked grouse meat with Philadelphia cheese and some black pepper.

Serves 4 to 6.

ROAST YOUNG GROUSE

Ingredients:
brace of young grouse;
2 slices of bacon;
50 g/2 oz butter;
2 slices of white bread, sautéed in additional butter.

Prepare the birds and put a piece of butter into each bird. Cover the breasts with bacon and put on a slice of well-buttered bread. Put into a roasting tin in a moderate oven, 375 deg F/190 deg C/Gas 5, for about 40 minutes, depending upon the size of the birds. Remove the bacon 10 minutes before the grouse are ready to allow the breasts to brown. Serve with bread sauce, fried breadcrumbs and gravy, also some crisps.

Grouse are sometimes served on a piece of fried bread on which the mashed liver of the birds has been spread. Cold roast grouse are delicious: if you want to serve them cold undercook by about five minutes, as they will continue to cook a little as they cool.

—Beef—

THE Aberdeen Angus breed of cattle has been celebrated for generations for yielding beef which is tender, succulent and full-flavoured, and discerning foodies everywhere have come to appreciate its distinct, marbled appearance due to the fine threads of creamy-white fat interwoven within the meat. This marbling effect on a joint of good beef is nature at its best, as this delicately flavoured fat helps to baste the meat from the inside. The result is succulent and tender beef.

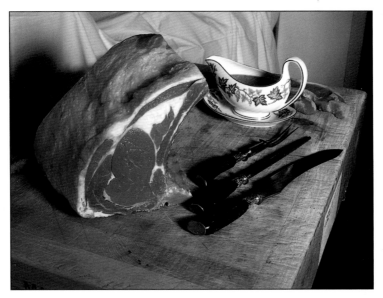

Did you know that the word 'sirloin' is said to have originated with King Charles II, when he returned to the hospitable mansion of Friday Hall at Chingford, Essex, after a day's hunting in Epping Forest? On entering the dining hall he beheld with delight a huge loin of beef steaming upon the table.

"A noble joint!" exclaimed the king. "It shall have a title!" Then, drawing his sword, he raised it above the meat and cried, with mock dignity: "Loin, we dub thee knight; henceforward be Sir Loin!" Whether this is true or not — and I believe it probably is — there is no doubt that throughout Europe, whenever there is a choice, beef is the preferred meat.

For generations eating beef conferred social status, and above all the English loved roast beef, well seasoned with "the taste of fire". The plainest of our English cooks could always turn out a beautiful roast, flanked by its traditional accompaniments.

Yorkshire pudding and horseradish sauce are essential accompaniments to roast beef. If you buy beef on the bone allow 8 to 10 oz per person; for steaks 5 to 6 oz per person.

Look for lean flesh which should be red and marbled with fat, firm and slightly moist. The fat should be cream or slightly yellow and firm, but not hard. Dark red meat with gristle under a layer of yellow fat is from an old animal and will be tough. Very red meat may also be tough because it has not been hung long enough.

The choicest cut is the sirloin and, roasted on the bone, this joint has the best flavour. Steaks are small portions (or should be) from choice cuts of beef — they are expensive but are tender enough to grill or fry and there is no waste. Second to a roast of beef, I recommend a beef steak pudding.

ROAST BEEF AND YORKSHIRE PUDDING

Ingredients:
1.6-1.8 kg/3 1/2-4 lb joint of beef;
2 tablespoons dripping or lard.
For the Yorkshire pudding:
100-125 g/4 oz plain flour;
1 large egg;
1/2 pint milk;
2 tablespoons cold water;
a little salt.

Wipe the joint and put it in a roasting tin with the dripping. Put in a pre-heated oven for 15 minutes, then reduce the oven temperature to 375 deg F/190 deg C/ Gas 5. Continue roasting the meat for a further 15 minutes per pound for rare beef and 20 minutes per pound for those who like it less rare.

To make the Yorkshire pudding, sieve the flour and salt into a large basin and make a well in the centre. Break the egg into the well and add a little of the milk. With a wooden spoon, gradually draw in the flour and mix the ingredients together, adding milk a little at a time until you have a thick batter. Beat with a wooden spoon until the batter is smooth, then stir in the remaining milk. Leave the mix to stand for about one hour or until the meat is cooked.

Remove the joint from the oven and keep it hot, then increase oven temperature to 450 deg F/230 deg C/Gas 8. Cover the bottom of a baking tin with a thin layer of fat from the roasting tin and put in the oven until it is smoking hot. Quickly stir the batter, and pour into the tin. Bake on the top shelf of the pre-heated oven for 20 minutes, until risen, crisp and golden brown.

Small Yorkshire puddings made in a bun tray are now sometimes preferred to one large pudding, especially where there are children. Roast potatoes, gravy and a green vegetable are the usual accompaniments.

Serves 6 to 8.

BEEF STEAK PUDDING

Ingredients:
450 g/1 lb suet crust;
1 tablespoon flour;
750 g/1 1/2 lb rump steak, cut into small thin slices, trimmed of fat;
4 shallots or 1 small onion;
120 g/1/4 lb mushrooms, sliced;
150 ml/1/4 pint red wine;
salt and black pepper.

Roll out the suet crust about 3/4 inch thick. Line a 2-pint bowl so that the crust stands up about 1/4 inch above the top. Roll out a circle for the top. Season the flour with salt and pepper and dip the steak pieces in it.

Put half the meat in the bowl, add the shallots or onion and pile on the rest of the steak with the mushrooms on top. Mix the wine with 1/4 pint of water and fill up to within 1/4 inch of the top of the bowl. Moisten the edge of the crust and press the lid on it. Cover with foil and then with a saucer or plate. Stand the bowl in a steamer or a pan of boiling water (the water should come halfway up the sides of the bowl). Cover the pan and simmer for three to four hours, adding a little boiling water as necessary to the pan.

——Salmon——

AS well as being the aristocrat among fish, salmon is versatile and easy to cook, delicious hot or cold. My father always said that the tail-end piece was best and unless I can have a whole salmon, I would agree with him.

You can buy fresh salmon at Seahouses and Craster and probably in other places on our coast as well. When choosing a fish check for firm, bright, silvery, sweet-smelling skin. The gills should be red and the eyes still bright. Sunken dull eyes, soft flesh that will take a thumb identification, brownish gills and a fishy smell denote a lack of freshness.

Depending upon how you plan to serve the salmon, either leave the head and tail on or cut off the tail, then the head just above the collar bone. Wash the inside of the fish out under running cold water, removing all blood or left-over membranes.

Whether you caught or bought your salmon, it is very simple to cook. The essentials are silver cooking foil and an oven. For cold salmon, oil the inner side of the foil; for hot salmon use either butter or oil — but a bland oil like sunflower.

Bake the fish for approximately 15 minutes to the pound in a moderate oven. I like to add a few herbs — dill or fennel preferably, otherwise bay leaves or a stick of celery. Lemon slices are also part of the embellishments, but arrange these on the salmon when it is cooked. A splash of dry white wine can go in the cooking parcel, making a juice for spooning over the salmon at serving.

A perfectly cooked salmon should flake away from the bone and no more. Even the most inexperienced cook can prepare a salmon if they follow these simple guidelines and don't overcook.

Fishmongers tend to cut steaks too thin; they should be at least three-quarters of an inch thick or they dry out. Season the steaks with salt and pepper and brush with oil or melted butter. Baste frequently and serve with either lemon or parsley butter, or mustard butter made with a spoonful of Dijon mustard. Traditional sauce accompaniments for salmon are hollandaise, green mousseline, bechamel, velouté or mayonnaise.

KEDGEREE

Ingredients:
175 g/6 oz flaked cooked salmon;
2 hard-boiled eggs;
1 chicken stock cube;
225 g/8 oz long grain rice;
100 g/3-4 oz butter;
150 ml/5 fl oz/1/4 pint cream;
1 small finely chopped onion;
teaspoon curry powder, pinch of nutmeg,
pinch of saffron (optional);
chopped parsley.

Dissolve the stock cube in a pan of boiling water and add the saffron if you want to use it. Otherwise substitute nutmeg, but add it later. Then put in the rice and cook for 10 minutes, until tender. Drain. Melt the butter in a pan, add the onion, cook gently for five minutes. Add curry powder, stir in the cooked rice, the fish and the chopped hard-boiled eggs. Fold in the cream.

Put the kedgeree in a buttered oven-proof dish, cover and put in a moderate oven for about 25-30 minutes to warm through. Just before serving, fork in the finely chopped parsley. A very good recipe for using up left-over salmon.

SALMON MOUSSE

Ingredients:
225 g/1/2 lb cooked salmon or 1/4 smoked salmon;
10 g/1/2 oz gelatine;
4 tablespoons boiling water or fish stock;
1 tablespoon sherry;
350 g/12 oz cottage cheese;
2 egg whites;
lemon juice;
salt and pepper.

For years I couldn't risk wasting salmon trying to make a mousse because I'm not clever with gelatine. Then I found this recipe which is very easy and very good.

Put the boiling water or fish stock into the liquidiser and add the gelatine and blend one minute. Then add the flaked fish, lemon juice, sherry and cottage cheese. Cover and blend again until well mixed. Turn out and add the stiffly beaten egg whites. Pour into a soufflé dish or individual ramekins and leave to set in a cold place.

BAKED SALMON STEAKS

Ingredients:
2 salmon steaks (about 2 ins thick);
300 ml/10 fl oz/¹/₂ pint fresh cream;
1 tablespoon lemon juice;
1 tablespoon chopped dill leaves;
1¹/₂ tablespoons Dijon mustard (optional);
chopped parsley.

Choose nice thick steaks because they will bake better. I find one large one will feed two people, but it is easier to dish up one smaller one each. Depending upon the size of the steaks, vary the cooking time. Sprinkle the steaks with a little salt and put them in a baking dish. Mix the other ingredients together, except the parsley, and pour over the steaks. Put in a moderate oven: 350 deg F/180 deg C/Gas 4. The steaks will take about 30 minutes. When cooked, sprinkle with parsley.

Pigeon

PIGEONS were once a staple of the national menu, and even middling establishments kept dovecotes for the kitchen. The Romans loved them. Pigeon was dish of the day for Louis XIV, who liked them especially served with peas.

Mrs Beeton recommends cold pigeon pie, seasoned and stuffed with *foie gras* and truffles and padded out with plovers' eggs and forcemeat.

But for readers who haven't a clue how to cook one of these birds (the wood pigeon — not its town-bred cousin), here are some straightforward recipes and tips on how to deal with them.

Most of the flesh on a pigeon is on the breast and they are annoying birds to pluck. The feathers come out easily enough — they almost float off — but then they go on floating and get into everything. Plucking pigeon is a job best done outdoors, provided that there is no breeze.

There is no close-season for pigeons, but they are more plump and fat when they have been living off the farmers' fields, best between May and October. Young pigeon have round breasts and soft, pink legs and I think wood pigeons do make the best eating; they can be distinguished by the white ring around their necks. You don't need to hang a pigeon, but I do like to empty the crop as soon as possible.

Pigeon give a rich, gutsy stock which can be used for soup. They go well with olives, but I don't care for olives so I haven't tried out a recipe using them. I'm too selfish to cook a dish which I can't taste myself. Cabbage is a traditional accompaniment and I often serve rice instead of potatoes.

PIGEON PIE

Ingredients:

3 pigeons (or 8 pigeon breasts);
440 g/1 lb rump steak;
seasoned flour and some oil;
110 g/4 oz chopped bacon or ham;
2 hard boiled eggs;
salt and pepper;
parsley;
220 g/8 oz flaky pastry;
850 ml/28 fl oz/1 1/2 pints good stock;
1 teaspoon Worcestershire sauce.

The mistake people make with pigeon pie is to omit the steak; it is important. Cut the meat into small pieces, roll in seasoned flour and brown in hot oil in a frying pan.

Put this on the bottom of a large pie dish. Place the pigeon flesh on top and then the bacon or ham, thickly sliced eggs, salt, pepper and parsley. Pour in 2 tablespoonfuls of water. Cover with flaky pastry, leaving a hole in the centre.

Bake for 2 hours in a moderate oven, 350 deg F/180 deg C/Gas 4. Before serving, fill up with a little boiling stock to which you have added the Worcestershire sauce.

Serves 4.

ROAST PIGEON

Ingredients:
4 young pigeons (only young, plump birds are worth roasting);
8 slices of pork fat or streaky bacon;
110 g/4 oz butter;
1 tablespoon chopped parsley or mixed herbs;
flour;
salt and pepper.

Mix the parsley or herbs with half of the butter, add some salt and pepper and put a lump in each bird. Truss and cover the birds closely with pork or bacon. Place in a pre-heated oven, 400 deg F/200 deg C/Gas 6, for about 25 minutes. Baste frequently with the remaining butter. Before serving, remove the fat, sprinkle with some flour and put the pigeons back in the oven to brown.

Serves 4 (one bird per helping).

CASSEROLE OF PIGEON

Ingredients:
2 pigeons;
300 ml/10 fl oz/$^1/_2$ pint of stock;
1 tablespoon white wine;
110 g/4 oz rice;
3 carrots and a bay leaf;
2 rashers of bacon;
salt and pepper.

Soak the pigeons in salted water for half an hour, then put them whole in a casserole with the stock, rice and sliced carrots. Add the bay leaf, wine and seasoning to taste. Cook, covered, in a slow oven for three hours. Add the bacon, chopped, after two hours and, if necessary, a little more hot stock. Serve this with redcurrant jelly and with a little nutmeg and a knob of butter added before serving.

Serves 3 to 4.

Winter

November is when I make my Christmas puddings and cake, and cook goodies for our church fair, so time spent in the kitchen is at a premium.

There are the festive bird and the ham to prepare, as well as the soup pot to get out so that I can use up the last of the garden vegetables. These may be the shortest and darkest days of the year but the cook will have more than enough to do. Make use of the freezer to save time and energy before the Christmas festivities. Soups and casseroles can be made in advance and are a boon to keep in reserve.

Goose

THE goose's association with feasts and festivities can be traced down the ages, so the bird is the number one choice for traditionalists.

Until the 16th century, goose was the peasants' fare. Swans and peacocks were eaten by rich families who, with aristocratic stoicism, put up with the near inedibility of the flesh of these birds in exchange for their beautifully ornamented appearances on their dining tables.

A goose was only served looking festive when it was accompanied by delicious stuffing. It was not until the 18th century that onion, sage and apple became the traditional stuffing; the inclusion of apples counteracts greasiness.

A typical banquet would have the dishes all on the table at once — entrées, soups, starters, main meat and vegetables. Only the sweets and puddings were served separately, as we do now.

To some people, goose means only one thing — *foie gras.* Others have an inbuilt prejudice, refusing to cook or eat the bird, believing it to be tough and tasteless. If you have had a bad experience with a goose, try it again.

Choose a quality, fresh, young bird. In northern England, farmers used to keep goose fat for rubbing on to the chests of ailing cattle; I wonder whether they still do this?

The fat which comes off a goose during cooking is luscious: thick and white, excellent for roasting parsnips and potatoes, and it keeps well for a long time. Goose is naturally fatty, but there is a tendency for the breast meat to dry out, so it must not be overcooked or the flavour will be spoiled and the flesh toughened. Keep a sharp eye on it, as you would do when cooking a piece of ham.

Unlike turkey, which becomes rather dry and dreary eaten cold for the second or third meal, cold goose makes flavoursome cold eating. A young goose is not always stuffed, although I do stuff mine — and the stuffing gets eaten very speedily. Traditionally, the bird needs a sharp, fruity stuffing — apples, dates and lemon are particularly good. Braised celery makes a good accompanying vegetable.

Young geese are known as green geese or stubble geese in northern England and Scotland. A goose looks a big bird but in fact, once cooked, it will not stretch to the same numbers as a turkey — do not be deceived into thinking you can feed a lot of people off a 10-12 lb young goose. There is no depth of flesh to be carved off the breast, and nothing underneath to carve either. But goose meat is rich, as opposed to turkey and chicken which is not, so diners do not need more than two or three slices each.

CASSEROLED GOOSE

A wild goose of doubtful age will need to be stewed. I am sometimes presented with one from the wildfowlers, and even our small grandchildren eat this casserole.

Ingredients:
1 large goose, or 2 small geese;
1 onion;
1 stick of celery; 1 bay leaf; 2 sprigs of thyme;
butter, cornflour and black pepper;
approx 300 ml/10 fl oz/$^1/_2$ pint red wine;
1 tablespoon redcurrant jelly.

Push the onion and the stick of celery inside the bird/s and truss the legs well together. Brown the goose/geese in a mixture of oil and butter in the casserole that you plan to use.

Leave the goose/geese breast-side down and pour the red wine over; then put in the bay leaf, some pepper and the thyme.

Bring to a simmer and put in a slow oven for about two hours, basting occasionally. When the goose is cooked, strain off the juices. Melt the redcurrant jelly in the juices and thicken slightly with cornflour mixed with water. If you haven't got redcurrant, use bramble jelly.

This recipe can be varied by adding sautéed onions or crème fraiche to the sauce. If the children are to be eating the casserole, I strip the best of the meat off the bird and casserole it like that. The goose carcase is excellent for stock and soup.

Serves 6 to 8.

ROAST GOOSE

Ingredients:

1 young goose;

1 apple, sliced and peeled, and some orange juice;

2 teaspoons sage or mixed herbs;

150 g/4-6 oz chopped walnuts;

rind and juice of half a lemon;

225 g/8 oz breadcrumbs;

1 beaten egg, melted butter, salt and pepper.

Stuff the goose at the neck and put the rest in the body cavity. Or, if you prefer, roll the stuffing into balls and serve these separately. Truss the goose, keeping the legs and wings in as close as possible to the body. Rub the bird all over with some butter.

Roast the goose breast-side down, turning occasionally. Cook at approximately 450 deg F/230 deg C/Gas 8 for 10 minutes and then turn down to 325 deg F/170 deg C/Gas 3 for a further two hours approximately.

Baste frequently, adding orange juice or some wine to the basting liquid. If you want to make gravy with the liquid in which the bird has been cooked, skim off some of the fat juices first. If I have some honey left in a jar, I smear this over the goose and cut down on the butter as it gives a crisp skin.

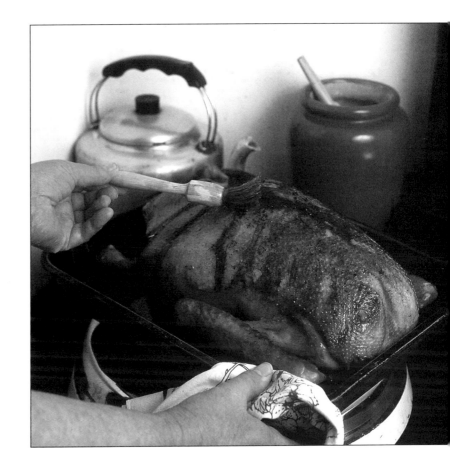

Christmas Cake and Pudding

LIKE most of us (excluding the children), I am thankful that Christmas comes but once a year.

It is essential to start planning early, and in these days of both parties working and time being increasingly of the essence, mail order has the edge. All sorts of goodies are available for the gourmet and the wine buff.

Christmas is geared to food but, with planning, much can be done in advance. One of the pitfalls is that people embark on elaborate meals when this is not the time to be too adventurous with the canapés. Simplicity is the key. You, too,

want to be dazzling and amusing, not a frazzled wreck stuck in the kitchen.

Keep menus simple — traditional Yuletide fare is rich and filling and there are likely to be edible gifts of crystallised fruits, chocs and biscuits. Plan ahead and freeze the turkey (or goose) stuffing and the bread sauce; you can even make the gravy two days ahead.

Should there be a large number of guests for the Christmas meal, prepare a lasagne: it makes a good contrast to the bird, and some people, especially children, may prefer it. It needs only to be accompanied by garlic bread or green salad and is ideal for Boxing Day.

CHRISTMAS PUDDING

Ingredients:
350 g/12 oz white breadcrumbs;
350 g/12 oz plain flour and 1 teaspoon salt;
$^1/_2$ teaspoon each of mace, ground ginger, nutmeg and cinnamon;
350 g/12 oz suet;
225 g/8 oz each of soft brown sugar and caster sugar;
225 g/8 oz chopped candied peel;
350 g/12 oz currants and 8 oz sultanas;
600 g/1 lb 4 oz raisins;
175 g/6 oz chopped, blanched almonds;
225 g/$^1/_2$ lb peeled and chopped apples;
grated rind and juice of one lemon and one orange;
4 tablespoons of brandy;
3 large eggs and 150 ml/5 fl oz/$^1/_4$ pint milk.

Mix all the dry ingredients in a large mixing bowl as well as the almonds, apples, and orange and lemon rind. Mix the lemon and orange juice and the brandy with the beaten eggs and add to the dry ingredients, with enough milk to give a soft dropping consistency.

Cover the mixture and leave overnight, then steam in greased basins for five hours (for one-pint-sized basins) or seven to eight hours (for larger basins). Then allow the puds to cool, cover with fresh foil and store.

On the day of serving they will each need approximately two hours' more steaming: another hour or two won't matter, but a shorter time will not do. Serve with brandy or rum butter, a sweet white sauce or fresh cream.

NORTH COUNTRY CHRISTMAS LOAF

In the 1920s and early 1930s times were hard in many parts of the North, and it was then that Christmas loaf — which originated on Merseyside — was first baked as a substitute for Christmas cake. It still makes a good fruit loaf and should ideally be made a few weeks before Christmas. Apparently, after a week, Liverpudlian cooks poured ale over the cooked loaf to improve its texture, but I haven't tried that; it stands well on its own.

Ingredients:

110 g/4 oz lard; 110 g/4 oz soft brown sugar;
1 egg; 1 tablespoon black treacle;
225 g/8 oz strong white flour;
1 teaspoon salt and 1 teaspoon grated nutmeg;
2 teaspoons baking powder and 2 teaspoons mixed spice;
225 g/8 oz currants;
25 g/1 oz chopped dried peel;
For the ferment:
1 egg; 75 ml/2¹/₂ fl oz warm milk;
25 g/1 oz sugar and 12 g/¹/₂oz fresh yeast;
50 g/2 oz strong white flour.

Mix the beaten egg and the warm milk together in a bowl to give 150 ml/¹/₄ pint of liquid. Whisk the sugar, yeast and flour into the liquid until thoroughly blended. Cover with cling-film or a plastic bag and leave to rise in a warm place for 30 minutes. Then make the dough by creaming the fat, sugar and treacle together with a wooden spoon in a mixing bowl until light and fluffy.

Beat the egg into the mixture, then sieve in the flour, salt, baking powder, nutmeg and mixed spice. Mix well until the ingredients combine to make a smooth mixture. Then work in the currants, and peel until evenly distributed.

Divide the dough in half and shape each to fit a 450 g/1 lb loaf tin, warmed and greased. Cover with cling-film or put in a plastic bag and leave to rise in a warm place for 45 minutes. Bake in a pre-heated oven at 400 deg F/200 deg C/Gas 6 for 35-40 minutes. If you want a large loaf you can shape the dough to fit a 900 g/2 lb tin and bake for one hour.

JEAN COCKBURN'S CHRISTMAS CAKE

Ingredients:

225 g/8 oz butter; 225 g/8 oz dark brown sugar;
225 g/8 oz plain flour and 50 g/2 oz self-raising flour;
50 g/2 oz ground almonds and 2 teaspoons mixed spice;
110 g/4 oz cherries; 175 g/6 oz sultanas;
225 g/8 oz raisins and 225 g/8 oz currants;
50 g/2 oz mixed peel; 5 eggs.

Cream the butter and sugar until light and fluffy, then add the beaten eggs gradually. Fold in the flour with a metal spoon. Lastly, add fruit and flavouring and mix well. Bake in an eight-inch cake tin lined with greaseproof paper at 275 deg F/140 deg C/Gas 3 for one hour, and then reduce to 225 deg F/110 deg C/Gas 2 for another three hours.

Ham

WHETHER we have a turkey, a goose or game birds for Christmas, there would be cries of anguish from the family if I did not produce a home-cooked ham as well. It compliments the rich fare and is endlessly useful in the days which follow the festival itself.

The most versatile of basic food, ham can be served for breakfast, sliced thinly with scrambled eggs, put into rolls or sandwiched, or just eaten with baked potatoes and salad for lunch.

I order my ham from my local butcher, soak it, boil it and finish it off roasted in the oven. I give directions below, and I can assure you that it puts the supermarkets' wet, plastic variety in the shade, where it belongs.

Strictly speaking, ham is the hind part or angle of the knee from the leg of a pig, cut from the whole carcass. Curing is performed in a variety of ways, each district in Britain having its own peculiar treatment. These, however, relate to minor points.

Some of our North Country butchers still use old curing skills, and it is wonderful to see the ham joints hanging in rows in cool, airy rooms looking like slumbering bats suspended on the rafters. Some hams are hung up only to dry; others, after being dried, are removed to the smoke house.

A York ham, dry salt cured and lightly smoked, is our favourite. In the days when each household had its pig, tradition dictated that the animal should be killed when the moon had just begun to wane. This was not actually such an old wives' tale, since free-range pigs graze by moonlight and would be heavier after a week feeding in the light of the full moon. The slow process of countryside curing would then begin. For centuries the pig was the main meat animal of our North Country farmworkers, whose kitchen beams were adorned by ham being cured by the rising wood smoke from the open fire on the range.

York hams have the edge, and there are still firms which cure correctly. A friend in the Malton area who is a very good cook tells me that York ham should be brined, dried and aged in sawdust for three months, and that legend has it that the first sawdust to be used came from the oak beams which went into building York Minster. So you can think of that when you next enjoy a piece of York ham.

Certainly, their methods are very ancient and similar to the Roman recipe recorded in Italy in the 2nd century BC. The Romans in Britain would have had no difficulty with supplies of salt — the essential ingredient in the preserving process for ham and bacon — because this commodity had been available around our North East coast from the Celtic Iron Age onwards.

I make sure to have some cider in the house when I serve ham cooked in the recipe I give here. Pigs are partial to apples themselves, and many of them were let into the orchards in autumn where they rooted for the windfalls.

A whole ham is very heavy to lift in and out of my oven, so depending upon the number of people you have to feed, 10-12 lb is a good size for eight to 10 diners with plenty left over for other meals.

—POTATOES AND HAM GRATIN—

This is a useful dish for using left-over ham, but do not freeze it.

Ingredients:
350 g/³/₄ lb cooked ham;
900 g/2 lb potatoes;
110 g/¹/₄ lb mushrooms;
1 clove of garlic;
50 g/2 oz butter;
50 g/2 oz strong Cheddar cheese;
300 ml/10 fl oz/¹/₂ pint milk;
150 ml/5 fl oz/¹/₄ pint cream;
salt, pepper and nutmeg.

Rub a flat baking dish with a cut clove of garlic and some butter. Then put the crushed garlic in a pan with the milk and simmer. Grate the cheese, slice the mushrooms and set these aside. Cut the ham into slices or strips, slice the potatoes thinly and layer them in the dish with the ham, mushrooms, a seasoning of salt, pepper and a scrape of nutmeg.

Dot with butter and sprinkle with grated cheese. Continue these layers, finishing with potatoes. Pour over the hot milk (without the garlic) and the cream, and top with grated cheese and dabs of butter. Bake for about 40 minutes in a hot oven until golden.
Serves 4.

BOILED HAM

Buy a plain, salted ham for this recipe — or a sweet cured and smoked ham is even better.

Ingredients:
1 whole ham (this will weigh around 6 kg/14 lb, or one of 5kg/10-12 lb approx);
some root vegetables (leave the onion skins on);
300 ml/10 fl oz/$^{1}/_{2}$ pint cider;
225 g/$^{1}/_{2}$ lb approx black treacle;
1 teaspoon peppercorns;
2 whole apples;
a bunch of herbs (parsley, sage, thyme, bay leaf).

Put the ham to soak for 24 hours and change the water twice. Wash, but do not peel the vegetables and chop them roughly. Lay these in the bottom of a large stewpot, then lay the well-soaked ham on top. Add the cider, treacle, peppercorns, herbs and enough water to cover.

Chop the two apples and put them on top: no need to peel them. Bring the stewpot to the boil, then turn the heat down and simmer for about three to four hours. Simmer — don't boil fast or the ham will toughen. This will be delicious eaten hot, and served with apple sauce or pease pudding.

To eat it cold, allow the ham to cool in the liquid so that it re-imbibes its own juices. This is important to keep the ham succulent when cold. Then, when it is cold in the pot, take it out and remove its rind. Stick it with cloves, score it and sprinkle with brown sugar. I sprinkle on a few of my home-made breadcrumbs too. Then put the ham in a hot oven at 425 deg F/220 deg C/Gas 7 for 30 minutes to gild the crust.

————— Bread —————

BREAD-MAKING is a science and a craft and, during the last century, housewives never ceased making their own bread at home.

The craft is basically about understanding the interaction of four ingredients: flour, salt, yeast and water. It takes nothing else but a baker to make these into excellent bread and we are now turning again to those crafts which were the delights of our forebears.

Although no-one wants to go back to grinding wheat with a pestle and mortar, there is something special about the feel of warm, live, silky dough and the homely smell of baking coming from the oven, not to mention the incomparable taste of real fresh bread.

It was the Romans who introduced into Britain an oven in which brushwood was burned before being raked out, leaving the oven hot enough for baking. Previously, bread was baked round the fire, uncovered at first, but later covered by a clay pot or dome.

From medieval times a bread oven became a fixture in manors, large houses and monasteries, but not in the homes of peasants and poor families. They either continued to bake their bread as hearth cakes round their own fires, or took their dough to the local manor to be baked for them, and paid for the use of the oven with some of the bread which they had baked. Cakes developed from enriched breads, but not until the 17th century did recipes for cakes appear as we know them.

Nutritionists say we should eat more bread, and in particular urge us to eat more wholemeal bread because of its high fibre content. This is right, not only on the grounds of good health but also of good taste. It is not for nothing that I include the recipe for a plain wholemeal loaf to bake and eat on a day-in-day-out basis.

Probably the best-known local loaf is a stotty, also known as 'oven bottom' cake since it was traditionally baked on the oven floor.

Stotties were originally made from left-over dough in the days when everyone baked at home, the round flat bread-cake being introduced to the high street in the 1960s. There is confusion about precisely how the bread got its name, the most likely explanation being that it has something to do with the way the dough is bounced on the table as it is kneaded. To stot is Geordie for to bounce.

One lady in north Northumberland who still makes stotties regularly told me that she uses no fat or lard for her stotties, and that the name was derived because the loaves ought to be so light they would 'stot' (i.e. skim) over the Tyne.

FELTON SPICE LOAF

This traditional high tea loaf is especially good.
Ingredients:
110 g/4 oz self-raising flour;
110 g/4 oz butter and 110 g/4 oz sugar;
2 eggs;
50 g/2 oz ground almonds;
110 g/4 oz plain flour;
half teaspoon mixed spice;
50 g/2 oz candied peel;
175 g/6 oz sultanas;
a little milk.

Pre-heat the oven to 375 deg F/190 deg C/Gas 5. Cream the butter and sugar together until fairly light, then beat in the eggs one at a time. Fold in the ground almonds.

Sift the flours together and the mixed spice and fold in, then stir in the peel and sultanas and add enough milk to give a dropping consistency. Turn the mixture into a well-buttered tin and smooth the surface. Bake for 30-40 minutes. Cool for five minutes in the tin, then turn on to a wire rack. Serve sliced, plain or buttered.

WHOLEMEAL LOAF

Ingredients:
5 cups wholemeal flour;
30 g/1¹/₄ oz easy-blend or fresh yeast;
2 teaspoons salt;
450 ml/15 fl oz/³/₄ pint warm water;
1 tablespoon oil or 12g/¹/₂ oz butter.

Mix the dry ingredients in the bowl of a food mixer. Put the water into a jug and add the oil or butter. Add the contents of the jug to the dry ingredients and mix and knead to a smooth, elastic dough.

→

The dough should then be covered and set aside to rise until doubled in size. This will vary depending on the heat of your kitchen. Go by the size of the dough and not by the clock: beside the Aga or in the airing cupboard it takes only an hour; on a sunny window sill it will take two hours.

When the dough is well risen it will be puffy and soft. Knock it back to get rid of air pockets and knead it again to make it smooth and elastic.

These processes can be done electrically, but they are quick and easy to do by hand. Kneading dough means pummelling, pushing and stretching it — be as rough as you like.

Shape the dough into your loaf tins by dropping the dough into the tins and pushing down lightly round the sides to give the loaf a nicely-rounded top. The tin should be greased first and the dough should fill it between a half and two-thirds.

Slide the filled tins into a lightly greased polythene bag and set to rise again, which will take about half an hour. Then bake in a pre-heated oven at 425 deg F/220 deg C/Gas 7.

A loaf is ready when it begins to shrink away from the sides of the tin. When turned out, the loaf should sound hollow if tapped on the base, and then it should be returned to the oven for a few minutes after unmoulding to colour the sides and the underside. Always cool fresh bread on a wire rack: this allows steam to escape.

—Soups—

A GOOD cook in early 19th century Northumberland households was judged by her ability to prepare broth. Earlier, culinary limitations were imposed on North Country families by a single pot, a single meat source and local produce — characteristics which evolved in a hundred and one nourishing soups and broths, each with a particular identity and usually made from an abundant larder.

Beef, lamb, venison, hare, wild duck and probably wild boar were all available to local communities. The old kitchen habit of frugality was part of the husbandry of making stock out of bones. Stocking the larder and making nourishing broths and soups out of a few and simple ingredients were the criteria of a good housewife.

Today, our main-course soups are a refinement of the early pottages and broths and our first-course soups a further refinement to stimulate the appetite for courses to follow. The variety of soup permutations we know today stems from a rise in living standards, more sophisticated tastes and wider availability of ingredients. Now, when planning a meat or vegetable-based soup, I like to remember the ancient traditions of using what is available, good to taste and nutritionally appropriate.

The stock pot is the basis of a good soup. Fowl and meat bones are simmered for hours to extract the last drop of their flavour and goodness. The greatest nutritional value comes from gelatine and the best source of this is bones.

A friend points out to me that it's cheaper to use stock cubes than to make my own. Her economics may be sound but I belong to the school that favours stock making. Use raw or cooked fowl, carcases and the giblets. Some chefs boil the feet, skin them and put those in too, but I think that is too Scrooge-like.

Electric liquidisers have revolutionised soup making and save hours of labour, but thick broths and vegetable soups can be rendered rather bland and emulsified if the machine is run too long. Watch the soup carefully and switch off the power when the veg is still in small pieces unless you like a very even texture.

Hot soup must be served piping hot because as it cools it loses flavour and any fat in it floats to the top. Serve soup in pre-heated bowls. An attractive garnish converts a humble soup into elegant fare — try croutons, chopped parsley, chives, celery leaves or cream swirled on each serving and sprinkled with cayenne pepper or paprika. If you make a soup for freezing it is best not to season it because salt and pepper increase their flavour while frozen. Add them when you heat the soup for serving.

Good home-made soup sums up the virtues of country cooking and the best brews are made from the freshest ingredients in season, carefully chosen and simply cooked. Friendly food, made for sharing, wholesome unpretentious and delicious, it is also sensibly economical of the cook's time and budget.

BASIC STOCK

Roughly the proportions are 450 g/1 lb of solid ingredients to 2 litres/3$^{1}/_{2}$ pints of liquid.
Ingredients:
450 g/1 lb of bones and meat (beef, lamb, fowl, rabbit or any game);
2 litres/3$^{1}/_{2}$ pints cold water;
2 large carrots, 1 onion and 2 sticks of celery;
salt, 6 peppercorns and a bouquet garni.

Break up the bones if they are large and cut the meat into chunks.

Put them in a large, heavy-based pan with salt and water. Bring slowly to the boil, remove any surface scum, cover and leave simmering gently for about three hours.

Then add the vegetables, cover again and simmer for two hours. Strain the stock through a sieve, discard the veg and bones and leave the liquid in a bowl to get quite cold. Remove the fat from the surface and store in the fridge.

Soup made from the above stock has many permutations. One very good soup consists of making a roux with butter and flour and adding the stock slowly to make a thick liquid. Season with salt and pepper, add four tablespoons of port, one tablespoon redcurrant jelly and some small cooked pieces of venison or hare (not the pieces that have boiled for five hours in the stock). Serve very hot. Two slices of smoked bacon will also enhance this soup.

CREAM OF LEEK SOUP

Ingredients:
700 g/1$^{1}/_{2}$ lb leeks, washed and trimmed;
50 g/2 oz butter; 150 ml/5 fl oz/$^{1}/_{4}$ pint of double cream;
2 large onions, peeled and finely chopped;
3 sticks of celery with leaves, washed and chopped;
1 large potato, peeled and chopped;
1 tablespoon chopped parsley;
1.5 litres/2$^{1}/_{2}$ pints chicken stock;
salt and pepper.

Heat the butter in a large saucepan. Keep one small leek aside and chop up the rest. Add to the pan with the onion and celery and cook over a low heat for 10 to 15 minutes until soft and transparent. Add the potato and stir over a low heat until the butter has been absorbed. Add the parsley and gradually stir in the stock. Season with salt and pepper and bring to the boil.

Cover and simmer for about 30 minutes until the vegetables are soft. Blend to a smooth purée in the food processor and then return to a clean pan. Add the cream and heat through.

I like to stir in the sliced raw leek just before serving.

MUTTON AND LEEK BROTH

Ingredients:
110 g/4 oz pearl barley;
900 g/2 lb scrag end of mutton or lamb sliced;
175 g/6 oz diced carrot and 110 g/4 oz diced turnip or
swede;
1 stalk of celery and 1 chopped onion;
2 leeks, thinly sliced and with the green part discarded;
1/2 level teaspoon thyme, salt, pepper, sugar and chopped
parsley.

Wash and soak the barley for four hours. Drain and put it into a large pan. Cut off bits of fat and add the meat with 4½ pints of water. Bring to the boil, skim well, and leave to simmer gently for an hour. Add the carrot, turnip and swede, celery, onion and half of the leek. Also the thyme and a little seasoning. Simmer for a further hour; mutton will take longer than lamb, so be prepared to give it extra time. When the meat begins to part easily from the bone, remove the slices and discard the bones.

Cut the meat into convenient pieces and return to the broth. Skim off the surplus fat — this is most important if you are eating the soup straight away because mutton fat tastes nasty in a broth like this. Taste and adjust the seasoning, adding a little sugar to bring out the flavours. Stir in the rest of the leek, bring the soup to a bubbling boil and serve with the parsley scattered on the top. Very good served with wholemeal bread and butter. A filling soup and rightly described as a "meal-in-a-bowl".

CHICKEN SOUP
(made from left-overs)

Ingredients:
225 g/8 oz cooked chicken meat, or pheasant, skinned and
boned weight;
700 g/1½ lb potatoes;
700 g/1½ lbs leeks and 225 g/½ lb carrots;
50 g/2 oz butter or fat scraped from the top of chicken gravy;
sugar and a little dried tarragon;
chicken stock;
fresh parsley.

Peel the potatoes and cut into chunks. Slice the leeks thickly, green parts as well as the white, and slice the carrots thinly. Heat the butter or fat in a large saucepan over a low heat, add the vegetables and stir to coat them all over with fat. Cover the pan and cook gently for about five minutes, stirring occasionally. Add a good pinch of sugar and dried tarragon, a little salt and a good grind of black pepper. Pour on the stock, enough to make an approximate total amount of 1500 ml/ 50 fl oz/2½ pints (this will give six generous cups of liquid).

Bring to the boil and give a good stir, then cover the pan and simmer gently until the vegetables are half cooked. Add the chicken meat, cut into slivers and continue to simmer gently until the veg is cooked and the chicken thoroughly heated through. Before serving, check and adjust seasoning to taste and thin the broth with extra liquid if you like a more liquid soup. Stir in several handfuls of chopped fresh parsley and add a small handful of crisp fried croutons to serve.

Leeks

GARRISONS of soldiers patrolling Hadrian's Wall during harsh winters must have been grateful for the sustenance of this hardy bulbous perennial plant. Leeks provided vitamin C, which prevented scurvy.

One of six members of the onion family known in England in pre-Norman days, the *porleac* or garden leek was mentioned as a cultivated vegetable in the laws of Hywel Dda, a Welsh prince of the 10th century.

From the time of the Industrial Revolution to the present day, leeks have been instrumental in providing friendly competition between challenging growers. Nurturing flowers and vegetables helped to give purpose to life in colliery communities, like keeping whippets and racing pigeons which provided both solitude and a measure of companionship.

Growing leeks is a Geordie fever attacking chiefly men, but a few women become addicted too, and the disease knows no social boundaries. Doctors, teachers, redundant miners, butchers and the retired — all succumb to *Allium porrum 'exhibitionii',* which means cultivating leeks to exhibition standards. In lay terms, this means producing a veg of gargantuan proportions.

Cared for by a connoisseur, a leek can increase its weight over nine months by nine million times — a feat only exceeded by the human foetus. Some of the methods of cultivation are as varied as the individuals who grow them: the exhibitor must provide warmth, water, fertilisers, fungicides and pesticides in varying amounts and at critical times in a protected environment.

"Too much of one ingredient or insufficient of another can spell disaster," said one of my leek-growing friends who regularly leaves half a dozen green and white giant leeks on my

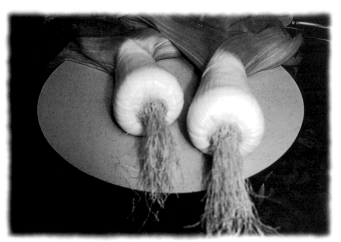

doorstep in the back end of the year. "You have to get it right so your leek is perfect for the day of the show. That's what counts."

During the months leading up to a leek show, money-raising events are held in order to swell the purse, and virtually every member of the relevant club seems to come away with something for his efforts. Ideal leeks should be 12 to 14 inches long with little or no bulbing, white for about two thirds of their length and with dark green foliage. Steady progress in leek breeding over the past decade has enabled growers to stretch the season at both ends, normally August until April.

Leeks have always been appreciated by the perceptive cook for their flavour and adaptability. For minimum wastage and tender eating choose leeks with long, thin white stems. Stout white parts are nearly always tough and the coarse greenery of leeks is not a pleasure to eat.

When the housekeeping budget is depleted for some reason or other, I turn to this economical and satisfying dish, given me by a Welsh cook.

Ingredients:
700 g/1$^{1/2}$ lb leeks, prepared weight;
75 g/3 oz butter;
1$^{1/2}$ (approx) eggs per person;
225 g/$^{1/2}$ lb cheddar,
or 110 g/$^{1/4}$ lb cheddar and 110 g/$^{1/4}$ lb Gruyère cheese;
3 slices wholemeal bread;
2 tablespoons plain flour;
1 pint milk.

Melt the butter in a large saucepan. Add the leeks, which must be thinly sliced, washed and dried. Turn until each piece is lightly coated with butter. Cover the pan and leave to cook gently for 15 minutes. In the meantime, hard-boil the eggs.

Put a large baking dish into the oven and switch it on to 375 deg F/190 deg C/Gas 5. Scald the milk, grate the cheese and reduce the bread to crumbs. When the leeks are tender, draw the pan away from the heat and sprinkle on the flour, then add the milk off the heat and return to the heat again bringing it to simmering, stirring gently to make a good sauce.

Slice the hard-boiled eggs and arrange in the hot dish, stir half the cheese into the leek sauce and season to taste. Then pour the sauce over the eggs, cover the dish with a lid or with foil and bake for 15 minutes until all the ingredients are piping hot.

Sprinkle the remaining grated cheese over the hot gratin and top with the breadcrumbs. Cook under a hot grill for a few minutes so that the cheese melts and the crumbs become toasted.

Serves 4.

LEEK PIE

This is a traditional North East recipe. The leeks set in the creamy custard along with the ham.

Ingredients:
450 g/1 lb leeks, cleaned and cut into 1-inch pieces;
short pastry;
225 g/$^{1/2}$ lb cooked ham or gammon rashers cut into pieces;
3 eggs;
150 ml/5 fl oz/$^{1/4}$ pint milk;
pepper.

Simmer the leeks in boiling salted water for five minutes. Drain and allow to cool for 10 minutes. Line a flan tin with the pastry rolled out to about $^{1/8}$ inch thick. Reserve a thinner circle for the lid.

Cover the bottom of the flan tin with the ham or gammon pieces. Beat the eggs and gradually beat in the milk and a pinch of pepper. Do not add salt, as the ham will salt the whole dish. Pour the mix over the ham and lay the cooled leeks in it. Put on the pastry lid and seal carefully. Brush over with the reserved egg and bake at 350 deg F/180 deg C/Gas 4 for about an hour.

Pheasant and Hare

THOSE of us who regularly cook game know how good it is and, especially today, how reasonably priced are pheasants in particular. Time was when pheasants were kept for special occasions, but no longer. They are now so plentiful and inexpensive that we eat them for supper rather than for dinner parties, and they adapt well to most chicken recipes.

We still pluck our birds but plenty of people do not, so there is no need to feel ashamed of skinning or taking a brace to the local butcher to prepare for you. Trussing any game bird is not as easy as trussing a domestic fowl which has had its neck wrung, rather than being shot. You come across wobbly legs and missing joints which won't fit where they should. Trussing keeps a bird neat: the legs and wings don't dry out, it looks more appetising and is easier to carve.

Hen pheasants make better eating than cocks and are much easier to pluck. A roasted cock will feed four people and a hen two or three, but if you have more mouths to feed you can cook the birds and use the flesh to make interesting dishes.

There are certain points to remember when choosing pheasants in the feather from a game dealer. Look for young birds with pointed flight feathers and smooth, pliant legs with short spurs on the male. Long spurs instantly give away an old trooper. Turn the feathers back to check that the breast is plump and firm and not peppered with shot. Pheasants should be hung singly by the neck in an airy cool place for about seven days. Some gourmets prefer them left even longer until the meat becomes strong and gamey.

A guide as to whether the pheasant is ready to pluck and cook is if the main tail feathers can be easily pulled out. If they come away without tugging, then start plucking. I pluck our birds into newspaper laid in the kitchen sink and make very little feathery mess, but even after years of practice, I cannot improve on 20 minutes' work for a hen and 30 minutes for a cock.

Two or three pheasants make a nice change from turkey at Christmas. Roast the birds, give them a waistcoat of bacon and some butter or a stuffing under the breast skin to prevent the flesh becoming too dry. It may sound like sacrilege to serve pheasant meat curried but I have had many compliments on this useful buffet lunch dish. It is also a good way to use up badly shot birds, old ones or those you skinned instead of plucking.

——STUFFED ROAST PHEASANT——

Ingredients:
1 pheasant;
110 g/4 oz butter or good fat;
50 g/2 oz sherry;
1 tablespoon redcurrant jelly;
juice ¹/2 lemon;
1 egg yolk, hard-boiled;
1 slice toast;
2 rashers of bacon.
Stuffing:
1 eating apple, skinned and chopped small;
5 tablespoons white breadcrumbs;
1 tablespoon chopped parsley;
1 lightly beaten egg;
2 tablespoons chopped bacon;
1 tablespoon chopped nuts;
1 teaspoon mixed herbs;
salt and freshly ground pepper.

Mix together all the stuffing ingredients. I often do this the day before because the ingredients bind together better and it is then easier to handle. If you have made too much it keeps well in the deep freeze for the next time. Stuff the neck end of the bird and sew or skewer the skin in place, then wrap the bacon over the breast. Smear butter all over the bird. Roast at 350 deg F/180 deg C/Gas 4 for about one hour.

Meanwhile, lightly fry the pheasant liver and process it to a paste with the yolk of the hard-boiled egg. Spread the toast with this paste and reserve on a hot dish in a warm oven. Just before the pheasant is finished roasting, drain off surplus fat from the roasting tin and pour the sherry over the bird and into the juices, then add the redcurrant jelly, lemon juice, salt and pepper and baste the bird well with this gravy.

Leave it in the oven another five minutes, or until you judge it just right, and then put the pheasant on the pâté-covered toast and serve as soon as possible.

Serves 3 to 4.

DEVILLED PHEASANT

Ingredients:
1 pheasant;
110 g/^{1}/$_4$ lb butter and 3 tablespoons good oil;
1 cup of double cream;
2 tablespoons chutney;
1-2 tablespoons Worcestershire sauce;
1^1/$_2$ teaspoons curry powder.

Pre-heat the oven to 400 deg F/200 deg C/Gas 6. Put the pheasant in a baking dish with the bird well buttered and the oil already hot in the dish. Turn the oven down to 350 deg F/180 deg C/Gas 4 and put the pheasant in for 10 minutes, then turn it on to its breast; baste every five minutes. It takes about 45 minutes. Don't over-cook or it may become hard.

When it is cold, cut the meat into bite-sized pieces. Whip the half pint of double cream. Add the chutney, Worcestershire sauce and curry powder to the cream and also some black pepper.

Put the pheasant pieces in this creamy mess and turn into the middle of a dish. Decorate with strips of ham. Surround with rice or cold sliced carrots. This dish is suitable for an *al fresco* supper.

Serves 3 to 4.

JUGGED HARE

Recipes for this vary because you can virtually put in what suits you or what you have to hand. It is correct to use a brown stoneware jug for the job, but ours is now broken so I use a heat-proof basin instead, which is just as good. This is the usual method I use:

Ingredients:
1 medium-sized hare;
110 g/4 oz rindless bacon;
110 g/4 oz chopped smoked ham;
6 shallots and 2 small onions, finely chopped;
150 ml/5 fl oz/^{1}/$_4$ pint dry red wine;
150 ml/5 fl oz/^{1}/$_4$ pint good stock;
juice of 1 Seville orange
or juice of half a lemon and half a sweet orange;
^{1}/$_2$ teaspoon ground mace;
4 cloves;
^{1}/$_4$ teaspoon grated nutmeg;
^{1}/$_4$ teaspoon grated lemon peel;
4 tablespoons plain flour;
butter for thickening, as much as needed;
salt and pepper;
150 ml/5 fl oz/^{1}/$_4$ pint hare's blood (optional).

Put the bacon, ham and shallots and onions, well mixed together, into the basin and add the wine, stock and orange juice, the herbs and spices and the lemon peel. Season the jointed hare with salt and pepper and put it in the mixture and cover the basin with a foil lid.

Put the basin in a pan with enough water to reach two-thirds of the way up the side and bring to the boil. Then simmer on a low heat for four hours, adding more boiling water as necessary to maintain the level.

Remove the pieces of hare meat and keep them warm on a serving dish. Allow the stock to cool and lift off the fat from the juices. Thicken the sauce with butter and a little flour or use the hare's blood if you wish. To do this you mix it with a teaspoon of flour to prevent it curdling and stir the blood into the juices.

Heat gently — too fast and the blood will curdle. Serve the hare in a casserole dish with the sauce poured over it and garnished with lemon slices and redcurrant jelly.

Serves 4.

FORCEMEAT FOR JUGGED HARE

Forcemeat, or stuffing, consists of a base to which fat, seasoning and herbs are added. The base is usually breadcrumbs or sausagemeat: for hare I make a mix of both and add the liver of the hare browned lightly in fat and chopped finely. Add chopped herbs — fresh if you have them. The texture should be crumbly but not wet. You have to get them just right because if they are sodden they will be heavy when cooked, and if they are too dry they will fall apart. Use a spoonful of the stock to bind them together. Forcemeat freezes well so can be made ahead of time.

Spring

*Spring means that inspiration in the kitchen rides high with new ideas and foods to be tried out.
Eggs, lamb and chicken are synonymous with Easter, but rabbits are also plentiful, and, of course,
delicious early vegetables.
Even if you are not a gardener yourself, you can usually buy most of the vegetables you need
at one of the excellent weekly markets now in our small towns. In this county we have wonderful cheese farms,
and spring is a good time to browse and buy soft cheeses.*

Lamb

SPRING months are prime time to enjoy lamb.

Shepherd communities have for generations relied on lamb and mutton from their flocks for sustenance.

The English and the Scots had their specialities. Jump-short pie was made from the unfortunate animals unable to climb the ravines or jump the gulleys, and braxy was mutton from the flock's casualties.

Lamb is meat from sheep which are three to 12 months old, while mutton is meat from animals 18 months to two years old. The flesh varies from pale pink to dark red, according to the age of the animal; mutton is darker red than beef and has more fat.

During the time of Queen Elizabeth I, sheep were so valued for their wool that they could only be eaten if they had died. It was not until the 16th century that lamb meat began to be enjoyed: until then beef had been the preferred choice.

Too often today, the only thing people look for when buying lamb is whether it is English or New Zealand. Home produced lamb is usually slightly paler and tastier than imported lamb, and where the fat on the joints should be hard and white, the fat on imported meat tends to be crumbly.

The choicest cut is the loin or back, with a leg or gigot a close second for succulence. There is not so much meat on the shoulder, but I think this tastes slightly sweeter than the leg. Braised shoulder of lamb is good too, boned and rolled and baked with carrots, celery and onions.

The recipe I give here for loin of lamb is one of my absolute stars, and can also be adapted to loin of venison.

When roasting a joint there are several common rules. Ten minutes per lb plus 15 minutes will yield rosy-pink meat; those who prefer lamb less rare will have a longer wait for its arrival. The first 25 minutes should be at high heat, 425 deg F/ 220 deg C/Gas 7, after which the temperature should be lowered to 350 deg F/180 deg C/Gas 4.

Do not add salt and pepper to the meat before cooking — the fat will melt and run off the meat too quickly. Instead add the seasoning halfway through cooking and baste the joint several times to keep it moist.

Navarins, stews and casseroles are good ways of dealing with older cuts of lamb since moisture and gentle heat coax the toughest meat to succulent tenderness. Mature mutton responds especially well. Shepherd's pie should be made with mutton mince from sheep, not beef mince. Why else would this traditional family dish be called 'shepherd's pie'?

For a celebration meal, ask your butcher to prepare a crown roast — two whole racks of lamb tied together with the meat on the inside and the bones on the outside to look like a crown. For best results roast this on its own, then fill it with a stuffing which has been cooked separately.

Traditional mint sauce is the perfect partner for roast lamb. Pull off the tough stalks from a large handful of fresh mint, roll these into a sausage shape and chop finely. Put in a bowl with one teaspoonful of caster sugar and one teaspoonful of boiling water. Add enough malt vinegar just to cover the chopped leaves and stir gently to mix.

To make a rich gravy to serve with roast lamb, first remove the cooked joint from the roasting pan and reserve. Skim off most of the fat, leaving a little with the pan juices. Stir in one tablespoon of flour and cook for one minute. Gradually add one wine glass of red wine and the same amount of lamb stock. Heat until bubbling, then simmer until slightly reduced and thickened. Stir in one teaspoonful of redcurrant jelly and season. Pour into a sauce boat to serve.

LOIN OF LAMB

Ingredients:

900g/2 lb loin of lamb, boned by the butcher;
1 chopped onion;
1 orange, grated and juiced;
3 tablespoons dripping or butter;
5 tablespoons soft breadcrumbs;
chopped parsley, rosemary and chives;
1 beaten egg and seasoning/flour;
1/3 white loaf, crusts off, reduced to fresh crumbs and
sautéed in a little butter or good oil.

Sauce:

1 sliced medium onion and half a pint of stock;
3 tablespoons redcurrant jelly;
a little orange juice;
parsley and watercress to garnish.

Make some stock from the bones taken from the loin of lamb by your butcher. To make the stuffing, soften the chopped onion in 1 oz of butter, add to the five tablespoons of crumbs with orange rind, herbs and seasonings, and then add the beaten egg to bind.

Season the meat with black pepper only, spread with stuffing, roll up and tie at intervals. Roll the lamb in flour, paint with egg wash, and roll in the browned crumbs, keeping the strings clear. Put in the fridge to set the stuffing. Cook the meat at 400 deg F/200 deg C/Gas 6 for about 45 minutes. Leave to rest in a very low oven and then cut off the strings which secure the roll.

To make the sauce, first check that the meat is cooked. Slide a knife into the meat: pink juices indicate that it is ready; red if it isn't ready; clear if it is overdone.

Remove the meat to a heated dish and put a little of the fat in which it was cooked into a pan. Add sliced onion and cook gently until browned and transparent. Add flour to take up any fat and stir to brown the flour but not burn it. Add hot lamb stock, whisking all the time, and cook for five minutes. Strain into a small pan, add redcurrant to taste and season. Finally, add orange juice but do not boil as it will lose its flavour. The juice is added to taste.

To serve, either slice the meat and pour a small amount of sauce along the centre of the presented slices without drowning them, or serve as a joint with the sauce in a small dish.

Serves 6 to 8.

Traditionally Irish stew really did hail from Ireland, and was usually made from mutton rather than lamb. Long cooking is the secret because Irish stew should never be watery.

Ingredients:
900 g/2 lb mutton or lamb;
1.8 kg/4 lb potatoes;
450 g/1 lb onions;
850 ml/1¹/2 pints stock or water;
salt and pepper.

Cut the mutton or lamb into pieces no more than one inch thick. Peel and slice the potatoes and onions. Reserve 1 lb of the potatoes, leaving them in salted water. Arrange in the casserole a layer of potatoes, then meat, then onion and finally a layer of potato, seasoning as you go.

Pour in the water or stock and cover with a lid. Cook in a slow oven for two hours. Half an hour before the end of cooking time, add the remaining slices of potato. Serve hot. Newcastle Brown Ale and a slice of local cheese go down well with this dish.

Irish stew can become hotpot by including a few chopped lamb kidneys and removing the lid for the last half hour of cooking to allow the top to brown.
Serves 8.

LAMB CHOPS WITH APPLE AND MUSTARD

Ingredients:
8 lamb chops;
1 onion, chopped;
1 tomato, sliced;
2 crushed cloves of garlic;
3 tablespoons good mustard;
1 tablespoon vegetable oil;
220 ml/8 fl oz apple juice (or white wine);
150 ml/¹/4 pint chicken stock;
freshly ground black pepper.

Heat the oil in a large frying pan. Add the onion, tomato and garlic and fry for about five to seven minutes until soft. Add the chops and brown on both sides. Mix together the mustard, apple juice and stock.

Season with the pepper, then add to the pan and stir well. Cover and cook for 15 minutes. Remove the lid and cook on a high heat for 10 minutes to reduce the sauce. Serve with potatoes and a vegetable of your choice. Use apple juice, but white wine makes a good substitute.
Serves 8.

Rabbit

RABBITS have been a crop-destroying pest since the first pair escaped from domestic warrens installed by the Romans in their encampments.

Today we still have a strain of black rabbits surviving on the Farne Islands which are descendants of those kept in captivity by early Christian settlers. During the Middle Ages, rabbit meat was esteemed above hare and leveret by cottage and castle, and the word 'rabbit' described an animal up to one year old. After that age it became a coney.

Buy from a game dealer and the beastie will be already skinned and jointed. If you buy it in the fur, look for a young animal with smooth sharp claws, soft papery ears and small, white teeth. An elderly rabbit will have dry ragged ears and probably blunt claws.

If I can't persuade anyone to skin for me, I arm myself with sharp scissors and cut open the belly of the rabbit up to the breastbone, then pull out all the internal organs and throw the entrails away. If the kidneys, liver and heart are undamaged I use them for stock. Ease the skin away from the flesh with the back legs held firmly in hand and pull the skin forwards towards the head, and ease it off the forelegs. Cut off the head.

Bought rabbit flesh can taste bland compared to the wild variety, so marinate it in soy sauce, lemon, brown sugar and bay leaves. Rabbits from old Northumbrian pasture which has been grass for as long as anyone can remember must be the most naturally fed animal you could eat.

RABBIT WITH CIDER AND WHISKY

Use young rabbits and adjust according to numbers: allow one rabbit to every four persons. Nowadays it might be wise to pick out all the bones as a sop to modern taste, although the original recipe leaves the diner to do this.

Ingredients:
1 rabbit, jointed;
350 g/³/4 lb mushrooms;
350 ml/12 fl oz (or 1¹/2 cups) dry cider;
3-4 tablespoons whisky;
300 ml/10 fl oz/¹/2 pint double cream;
25 g/1 oz butter;
fresh parsley and coriander seeds.

Shake some pepper and salt and the coriander seeds over the rabbit, then seal the meat in butter in a hot frying pan. Transfer the browned rabbit to a casserole in which you have already heated the cider. Cover it and cook at 300 deg F/150 deg C/Gas 2 until the meat is tender. 1¹/2 hours should be right for farmed rabbit; wild rabbit will need longer.

Transfer the cooked rabbit to a warmed serving dish and keep warm. Reduce the cidery liquid to less than half the quantity by fast boiling. While this is reducing, sauté the sliced mushrooms in the original frying pan, adding more butter as necessary. Arrange the mushrooms over the meat and season again with salt, pepper and coriander.

Pour the reduced cider into the frying pan, add the whisky and flambé. When the flames have died down, pour on the cream. Return to the pan and cook gently, stirring continuously until it is all smoothly blended and the sauce is bubbling and slightly thickened; this should take no more than five minutes.

Season the sauce to taste, pour it over the rabbit, cover again and return to the oven for 15 to 20 minutes before serving. This is a rich casserole which should be garnished with chopped parsley and served either with small baked potatoes or boiled rice.

Serves 4.

RABBIT PIE

Ingredients:
1 or 2 young rabbits;
225 g/8 oz puff pastry or flaky pastry;
1 chopped onion and some diced bacon;
75 g/3 oz mushrooms;
75 g/3 oz butter;
300 ml/10 fl oz/¹/2 pint of good stock;
2 hard boiled eggs;
salt and pepper.

Joint the rabbits and cut the flesh off the bone into bite-sized pieces. Sauté the onion and bacon in the butter, then add the rabbit to the pan, season and add the stock. Simmer gently for 45 minutes and then leave to cool.

Turn the rabbit mixture into a pie dish with a funnel in the centre and surround it with sliced hard boiled eggs. Place pastry lid on top, brush with egg and cook for 35 minutes at 400 deg F/200 deg C/Gas 6. Reduce the heat and cook for 15 minutes longer.

Serves 4.

RABBIT CASSEROLE

This rabbit casserole was served to me by a friend in Devon. It was delicious and she gave me the recipe.

Ingredients:
450 g/1 lb rabbit pieces, either jointed or meat only;
1 shredded Savoy cabbage;
6 rashers bacon;
150 ml/5 fl oz/½ pint dry white wine;
2 tablespoons olive oil;
25g/1 oz butter;
1 tablespoon chopped parsley;
2 cloves garlic, thinly sliced.

Put the cabbage in the base of a greased casserole dish. Heat the oil and butter in a large frying pan and fry the rabbit pieces until golden. Arrange the rabbit on top of the cabbage and sprinkle over parsley and garlic. Add about 4 tablespoons of water to the frying pan with the wine, bring to the boil, then pour this over the rabbit. The liquid should just cover the cabbage; add more wine if necessary (I usually need to).

Cover with the bacon rashers, replace the lid and bake for one hour at 350 deg F/180 deg C/Gas 4. Then remove the lid and cook for another half-hour to crisp the bacon. This is good with baked potatoes and carrots, broccoli or sprouts.

Serves 4.

—Venison—

VENISON is one of the best value meats on the market and one of the healthiest. It has a rich, rounded flavour, deeper than beef and mutton, and punchier than the game birds. At one time all our home-produced venison was shipped to Germany, but foodies in Britain have woken up to what they were missing and the meat has claimed many converts.

European Union rules improved conditions in deer stalkers' game larders, which in many cases left a lot to be desired. Farmed deer have also improved in quality and venison is now sold to stringent standards of hygiene.

There are five species of deer in Britain — red, roe, fallow, muntjac and Chinese water deer — and connoisseurs profess to be able to differentiate the taste between them. All are delicious but meat from an old beast or a male one during the rut are best avoided.

Venison has little fat and must be well larded with dripping or butter for roasting, but there is minimal waste. The meat freezes well. Never overcook — generations of cooks have rendered venison joints tough and tasteless by doing this.

During cooking, a joint can shrink deceptively. I used to panic when I took a haunch out of the oven and saw my dinner party delicacy honing from the bone, but once the carver got busy I could see that there was plenty to go around.

It is solid meat and should be sliced thinly and served on really hot plates or it quickly looks grey and unappetising. It will taste fine, but visual impact is important, especially for guests new to the meat.

Marinating is not essential but for a special occasion a marinade is probably advisable. My standard one is: half a bottle of red wine, 1 sliced onion, 1 clove of garlic, 3 tablespoons of good olive oil, 3 tablespoons of brandy, salt, pepper and some herbs (parsley stalks, thyme and a bay leaf). You can lay the venison in this cold, or heat the marinade gently until it is hot (not boiling) and pour on to the joint. Soak for up to 48 hours.

Here in Northumberland, we hang our deer for anything up to 10 days, but there is no hard and fast rule about this; it depends on the weather. We use roe deer which have been shot on local estates or red deer from the Highlands. Up-market butchers may offer superior cuts of venison at high prices: these are likely to be fallow in the South and Midlands, roe and red deer in the North.

If you know a game farm, pay a visit because they now sell well hung and prepared cuts of meat. Venison sausages are readily available. The liver and kidneys from a deer are considered to be the stalker's perks so game dealers do not often have them on the slab; snap them up if you do see them.

The kidneys are good on toast and I also keep them in pairs in bags in the freezer and use them for steak pies. The liver can be sliced and rolled in seasoned flour and then fried and casseroled with bacon and mushrooms. Liver is tastier from a young beast — never buy discoloured or damaged liver from a deer carcase.

To roast a haunch or loin of venison, lard it with strips of bacon for the last half hour of cooking — this improves the flavour and gives the meat an appetising pink tinge. Roast for approximately 20 minutes to the pound, basting frequently. Serve with redcurrant jelly and a gravy made with liquid from the marinade if you have used one, otherwise use some stock for this.

For a special occasion, I recommend a good red wine from Burgundy which will complement venison perfectly. You need a slightly plummy flavour, a touch of sweetness in the wine to set beside a haunch of venison.

VENISON LASAGNE

Ingredients:
150 g/5 oz green or white lasagne sheets;
225 g/8 oz (approx) minced venison meat;
2 tablespoons olive oil;
4 oz tomato purée;
1 clove garlic;
1 teaspoon dried oregano;
1/2 teaspoon dried basil;
400 g/14 oz tin of tomatoes;
350 g/3/4 lb Ricotta or curd cheese;
1 egg and a little milk;
110 g/4 oz Mozzarella cheese (or 8 oz Cheddar cheese)
60 g/2-3 oz mushrooms;
a little freshly grated Parmesan cheese;
a stick of celery, finely chopped (optional);
salt and pepper.

Brown the meat in the oil in a casserole. Add the garlic, finely chopped, the roughly chopped tomatoes and the tomato purée. Season all this, then add the herbs. Simmer for about 40 minutes.

Beat the Ricotta cheese and egg together until smooth, adding a little milk if necessary. Spread the gratin dish, well buttered, with meat sauce on the bottom and then layer up with lasagne sheets, the Ricotta cheese, thin slices of Mozzarella and the meat sauce. Sprinkle the top with Parmesan cheese if you have it. Bake it in a moderately hot oven for about 45 minutes until brown and bubbling.

Serves 6.

CRISP CHEESE PASTRY

Napoleon called us a nation of shopkeepers. He could equally well have described us as a nation of pastry cooks. This is easy to make and very good.

Ingredients:

175 g/6 oz butter or margarine;
150 g/5 oz grated mature Cheddar cheese;
2¹/2 cups self-raising flour;
¹/2 teaspoon each salt and mustard powder;
pinch of cayenne pepper;
6 tablespoons cold water.

Sift the flour, salt, mustard powder and cayenne and then grate the chilled butter or margarine on to the dry ingredients, and mix.

Stir in the cheese and mix to a firm dough with the cold water — very good for a savoury quiche pastry.

MACARONI CHEESE

Macaroni cheese is always a good stand-by meal and I have yet to meet someone who does not like it. The dish reached its height of popularity as a supper dish in Victorian times. The secret of success is to be lavish with a good strongly-flavoured cheese sauce. Visit one of our specialist cheese shops and ask for a suitable good melting variety.

Ingredients:

350 g/12 oz macaroni;
150 g/4-6 oz grated cheese;
25 g/1 oz butter;
25 g/1 oz flour;
15 fl oz/³/4 pint creamy milk;
salt and freshly ground pepper;
¹/4 teaspoon nutmeg;
25 g/1 oz breadcrumbs;
10 g/¹/2 oz butter cut into pieces.

Boil the macaroni in well-salted water for 15 to 20 minutes. Do not overcook or it will not absorb the sauce. Drain well. To make the cheese sauce, melt the butter in a medium saucepan, stir in the flour and let it cook for two minutes over gentle heat. Gradually add the milk, stirring all the time with a wooden spoon to obtain a smooth, creamy sauce. Season and add the nutmeg.

Let the sauce cook gently for 10 to 15 minutes, stirring from time to time, then add the cheese. When this has melted, stir in the cooked, drained macaroni. Pour the mixture into a pie dish and sprinkle the top with breadcrumbs, dot all over with butter and bake in a pre-heated medium oven for 20 minutes until golden brown.

Serves 4 to 5.

Index